W9-DHF-750

NEGOTIATING DISARMAMENT
The Eighteen Nation Disarmament Conference:
The First Two Years, 1962-64

by ARTHUR S. LALL

CENTER FOR INTERNATIONAL STUDIES
CORNELL UNIVERSITY
Ithaca, New York, 1964

To

OMAR LOUTFI

Acknowledgements

I am indebted to all my colleagues and friends at the Geneva Disarmament Conference without whose discussions, both in and outside the Conference, this work would not have been possible.

I am equally indebted to many friends at the United Nations, including U. Thant, Vladimir Suslov, Dragan Protitch, Arvind Vellodi, Bill Epstein, Amy Pierce and others through whose good offices I have continued to be well informed on the progress of the Geneva Conference since I left it late last summer.

Finally, I am grateful to Cornell University, and particularly the Center for International Studies, for encouraging me in this work.

CONTENTS

CHAPTER I

The Immediate Background

A. *The Colossus of Modern Weaponry*

In recent years the two major protagonists in the Cold War have been startlingly successful in building their military might. It is this mutual over-success which most nearly explains their sudden and relatively swift agreement on the principles (1) that should govern negotiations for a comprehensive program of disarmament, which was followed by an even swifter agreement on the composition of a negoatiating body. (2)

The immediate problem was the over-development of the thermonuclear weapon and both sides recognized this with the utmost clarity. Thus, in their joint message (3) to Mr. Khrushchev on February 7, 1962 on the eve of the Geneva 18-Nation Disarmament Conference, President Kennedy and Prime Minister Macmillan said: "The threatening nature of modern armaments is so appalling that we cannot regard this problem as a routine one or as an issue which may be useful primarily for the scoring of propaganda victories." In his reply, (4) dated February 10, 1962, Mr. Krushchev said: "And these questions are becoming a source of increasingly profound and grave concern to the peoples in that the armaments race is still growing, consuming the labor and wealth of hundreds of millions of people, while the threat of a new war is increasing, finding material expression in the massive accumulation of armaments."

The Geneva negotiations opened on March 14, 1962 with a vivid underscoring of this realization. President Kennedy's message to the Conference, read to us by Dean Rusk, stated, "Men know now that the amassing of destructive power does not beget security." (5)

---

(1) Joint statement of Agreed Principles for Disarmament Negotiations, tabled at the 18-Nation Conference by the delegations of the U.S.S.R. and the United States as document No. ENDC/5, Dated March 19, 1962, had already been welcomed in G.A. Res. 1722 (XVI), Part I, dated Dec. 20, 1961. See Annex to this study.

(2) G.A. Res. 1722 (XVI), Part II, par. 1, dated Dec. 20, 1961.

(3) ENDC/7, dated March 16, 1962.

(4) ENDC/8, dated March 19, 1962.

(5) ENDC/7, dated March 16, 1962.

Two days later, on March 16, 1962, Mr. Khrushchev said, "The destructive power of modern nuclear weapons, the possibility of their being dispatched to any point of the globe, today constitute such convincing arguments that human reason cannot help but demand as speedy as possible settlement of the disarmament problem." (6)

The nature of modern weaponry was clearly impelling the leaders of the two sides to send their representatives to the negotiating table. There were other stimulating factors at work.

B. *The Third World Comes of Age*

For the first seven years or so of United Nations history, the non-aligned countries were a small insignificant minority, and indeed they showed little inclination to involve themselves in what appeared to be a quarrel between ex-allies of World War II. But things suddenly changed. The success of the Indian resolution on Korea (7) altered the status of the nonaligned at the United Nations, and about the same time they had listened to enough of the wordy passages between the West and the Soviets to realize that the quarrel between those powers was such that it could sear and even destroy them in spite of the own non-involvement. In April 1954 Prime Minister Jawaharlal Nehru took a step which arose out of this new realization and made the world take note that the non-aligned were no longer going to remain on the side lines. He asked the United Nations (8) to put on its agenda the question of the cessation of nuclear weapon tests. Not that India or any other Asian country was testing, but that the tests posed a threat to the security of the whole world was the argument of the plea to the United Nations. Thus, it was a non-aligned initiative which brought to the United Nations the issue of nuclear tests.

Then, later in 1954, came the historic unanimous General Assembly resolution on disarmament (9)—the first to be supported by the Soviets since 1946. Part B of this resolution, also unanimously adopted, transmitted to the Disarmament Commission the whole draft of a resolution introduced by India and containing four disarmament proposals.

---

(6) Moscow Radio Broadcast, March 16, 1962. See U.S. Arms Control and Disarmament Agency, **Documents on Disarmament,** 1962, Vol. I, p. 151.

(7) G.A. Res. No. 610 (VII), dated Dec. 3, 1952.

(8) U.S. Department of State, **Documents on Disarmament,** 1945-59, Vol. I, pp. 408-413.

(9) G.A. Res. No. 808 (IX), dated Nov. 4, 1954.

Thus, from 1953-54 dates the emergence of a new posture at the United Nations. By 1957 this posture had gained so many adherents that the non-aligned countries and their friends could stop any other single group in the United Nations from getting its way—from mustering the requisite two-thirds vote for adoption of a resolution. From this time on there has been at the United Nations the floating uncommitted vote on which neither side can count. The debates on disarmament have ceased to be dialogues between the political West and East and have become world debates in which the two sides have been increasingly under pressure to justify their proposals and attitudes to the third world.

This new position was effectively demonstrated at the Fifteenth session of the UN General Assembly in the winter of 1960-61. That year there was a whole sheaf of draft resolutions on disarmament—as many as eight or nine. (10) This proliferation of texts was itself evidence of the aroused interest of the member States in the subject. A few years previously the pattern had been a Western draft resolution, which would be adopted by a majority vote, and a Soviet draft resolution, which would be rejected. However, the proliferation of drafts at the Fifteenth session also indicated a lack of agreement on what should be done. In these circumstances the West hoped that at least one or more of its drafts would be adopted—the tradition of the United Nations was to end the discussion on disarmament with at least one resolution adopted—even if no agreement had been reached which could command universal adherence. But at the Fifteenth session this was not to be. The nonaligned stood strongly against any move which would give the world the impression that the Assembly had put its seal on the position of one side or the other. In the end, not a single one of the sheaf of resolutions was adopted. I believe this fact was one of those that influenced the United States and the Soviets to make the bilateral moves which resulted in agreement on the principles for disarmament negotiations, and on a list of participants. That list now inevitably included a number of nonaligned countries. It was no longer possible to ignore them functionally, though in terms of military power they still remain of very limited significance: Their defense budgets total some $7.5 billion a year, out of a global figure of about $125 billion. Sweden is strong for her size but would not count significantly in a world conflict. India is still weak for her size in spite of the fact that after her unceremonious mauling by China her defense budget has jumped to about half the level of the three major European countries—France, the Federal Republic of Germany, and the United Kingdom—and exceeds the level of the defense expenditure of any other country except the nuclear powers and China. Though these are relevant indications of the military factors involved, the

---

(10) U. S. Department of State, **Documents on Disarmament** 1960, pp. 297-367.

nonaligned countries are now, by agreement, the largest group (though they do not and were not expected to function as such) at the Conference table. (11)

On December 13, 1961, Adlai Stevenson and Valerian Zorin introduced a joint U.S. Soviet draft resolution at the Sixteenth session of the UN General Assembly. The Assembly adopted it unanimously, (12) and in so doing welcomed the Joint Statement of Agreed Principles, (13) as well as the new Disarmament Committee consisting of negotiators from *Brazil,* Bulgaria, *Burma,* Canada, Czechoslavakia, *Ethiopia,* France, *India,* Italy, *Mexico, Nigeria,* Poland, Rumania, *Sweden,* Soviet Union, *United Arab Republic,* United Kingdom and the United States. (In this list the names of the nonaligned countries have been italicised.)

However, the nature of modern weaponry, and the pressures of the third world were not enough to lead to genuine negotiations. It was still possible to hold a purely talking conference, and after it had been in session for a few weeks or months, to close it down and indicate to the world that an effort had been made but no success had been possible.

C. *The Will to Negotiate*

Without a staunch will to negotiate no real discussions would be possible at Geneva. Is it now the case that such a will does impel the two sides and the nonaligned to negotiate with a view to alter the present precarious system of world security for something better and more acceptable to all countries? I believe it can be shown that this is substantially the case.

Let us take first the United States, by common consent the most heavily and potently armed of all countries, and therefore the one whose system of security stands to be most greatly altered by a new system of security. There are a number of relevant facts which indicate that both the major political parties in this country are behind the effort to achieve properly safeguarded disarmament. Mr. Arthur Dean, the first leader of the U.S. delegation to the 18-Nation Disarmament Conference, and his successor, Mr. William Foster, the Director of the U.S. Arms Control and Disarmament Agency, are both distinguished Republicans. Since they were sent to Geneva by an Administration that is Democratic one might reasonably conclude that the Democrats are, by and large, in favor of this type of effort, and furthermore, that it is considered desirable to express to the

---

(11) For a fuller treatment of the nonaligned in disarmament negotiations see the author's article in the May 1964 issue of the **Bulletin of the Atomic Scientists.**

(12) G.A. Res. 1722 (XVI), dated Dec. 20, 1961.

(13) ENDC/5 and Annex to this study.

nation and to the world the fact that there exists among the political parties substantial unity of will and purpose in this matter.

There are, of course, other facts which indicate the bi-partisan and national character of the United States' approach to the issue of disarmament. Thus, it was Senator John Sherman Cooper, again a Republican, who made an impassioned and successful plea for the retention of the word "Disarmament" in the title of the Agency at Washington which Mr. William Foster heads. Secondly, Mr. John J. McCloy, another distinguished Republican, led the U.S. team to negotiate the Agreed Principles for Disarmament with the U.S.S.R. To my personal knowledge he has won the genuine and deep respect of the Russian statesmen and diplomats with whom he has worked. (14)

It has fortunately come to be realized that disarmament is not a subject for unreal and naive "idealism." On the contrary, the peace-war stakes are now such that disarmament is of particular interest to those who would call themselves conservatives, inasmuch as they would want to ensure that the values and properties they respect or hold dear will not be destroyed in a brutal exchange of the power of modern weapons.

On the Soviet side I draw attention to a few relevant developments. The first of these is an important Communist statement intended for internal Communist consumption, not for propaganda in the non-Communist world. On June 14, 1963 the Central Committee of the Chinese Communist Party addressed a long communication to the Central Committee of the Soviet Communist Party which contained many statements hitting at the Soviet Party, in the following vein:

"Certain persons now actually hold that it is possible to bring about 'a world without weapons, without armed forces and without wars' through 'general and complete disarmament' while the system of imperialism and the exploitation of man by man still exists. This is sheer illusion." (15)

Such charges, which are made periodically, are evidence that the Chinese, who have had access to Party and Governmental leaders in the Soviet Union in a degree denied to most others, are convinced that the Soviet Union is in favor of disarmament and other similar moves in its relations with the West. This, I suggest, is fair evidence of the mood and will of the Soviet Union in the matter of disarmament negotiations.

---

(14) Attention could also be drawn to the strong bi-partisan Senate vote in favor of the Partial Test Ban Treaty. The Senate, on Sept. 26, 1963 approved 80 (Democrats 55, Republicans 25) to 19 (Democrats 11, Republicans 8).

(15) **New York Times,** International Edition, July 5, 1963.

There is another fact which most non-Communists who have been subjected to the experience I am about to cite will, in varying degrees, confirm. Meetings of the United Nations Conferences on the Peaceful Uses of Atomic Energy, (16) the Pugwash Conferences, or the Board of Governors of the International Atomic Energy Agency have, particularly recently, shown Soviet scientists, and those of such countries as Poland, as clearly interested in peaceful and agreed settlements with the West, and do not reveal an attempt to take over the world. Such views, while they do not establish any case, are some indication of the way trends are developing.

Finally, as representative of India at the Conference on the Question of Laos (1961-62), I was struck, as were many of the Western participants, by the constructive approaches and helpful attitude of the Soviet co-chairman of the Conference (the late Deputy Foreign Minister M. G. Pushkin). This was in contrast with the more belligerent attitude of the Chinese delegation from Peking, and contributed greatly to the reaching of accords at the Conference.

I believe there is evidence on the Soviet side of a will to negotiate agreements with the West and the rest of the world. This is, of course, far from saying that they are willing to accept Western or other approaches, particularly when they consider their vital interests to be involved. But wariness of this kind is common to all nations that sit down to negotiate, no matter how strong their good will toward each other.

As for the nonaligned, I have already given instances of their initiatives, and their general attitude toward disarmament, at the United Nations. At the same time, I wish to make it clear that I do not suggest that these countries are especially blessed with peaceful motivations. This is not the case. But there is nevertheless an enormously important (for them) practical factor which does predispose them toward disarmament. This is that most of these countries are woefully underdeveloped. Their people live in appalling conditions. Most of their leaders know that the people will not accept this state of affairs indefinitely. There is, therefore, a certain urgency about the adoption and implementation of developmental programs. These would be much more feasible and effective if a considerable part of the world's goods and technology, now absorbed by the defense efforts of the major Powers, could be diverted to development.

It would be too good to be true if the will to negotiate disarmament were universal. There is the attitude of France, not against disarmament, but showing an unwillingness to discuss it in the presently set up forum and in the present state of military superiority enjoyed by certain Powers. France, though a member of the 18-Nation Disarmament Committee, has

---

(16) It has been unanimously decided that the president of the third of these periodic Conferences is to be Vasily Emelyanov of the U.S.S.R.

never come to the negotiations. President de Gaulle explained France's dissociation from the Conference in a letter to Mr. Khrushchev on February 18, 1962. He wrote:

"In order to have a chance to succeed, it is, in my opinion, necessary that negotiations take place between the powers that possess nuclear weapons or that will possess them in the near future. One cannot see, indeed, how the participation of States that at present have no direct responsibility in this matter could lead to positive results. . . . In order to remove the danger and lighten the burden that nuclear weapons place on mankind, the essential question is not the halting of tests, but rather, as you yourself have often stated, the destruction of existing weapons and the banning of the manufacture of new ones. The halting of tests would in no way by itself constitute a beginning of disarmament, and the monopoly of the countries that possess nuclear weapons and that would keep this decisive means of domination in their possession would in no way be affected by this.

"It would also seem useless to me to want a destruction of weapons without a system of real control. . . . It is for this reason that France has unceasingly advocated that the destruction, and the banning and the control should first be applied to the means of delivery of nuclear weapons —launching pads, planes, submarines, etc.

". . . I wish to say that France is ready to participate in any talks that would be between the nuclear powers—the Soviet Union, the United States, Britain and France—and that would have as their immediate goal the destruction, the ban and control of all means of delivery of nuclear weapons. . . ." (17)

The Soviets adopted something of the philosophy of the General by giving priority, in their draft treaty on general and complete disarmament, to the elimination of the means of delivery of nuclear warheads. But, as we shall see as this study progresses, this is not a realistic approach and it has been abandoned by the Soviets.

As to the rest of the French position, it is, in a sense, an inducement to countries to join the nuclear club—for these will be the decision makers and they will be in a position to dominate the world. This view does not help disarmament forward. Besides, the non-nuclear countries would never assent to a thesis postulating that those countries which could use nuclear weapons against the non-nuclear world should decide how and when to divest themselves of their military might. Nor would it be reasonable to ask them to do so, particularly as even if they were non-belligerents in

(17) **New York Times**, February 20, 1962.

a big nuclear conflict their countries could suffer and perhaps be totally destroyed.

The Chinese approach has, to some extent, come out in the communication from the Chinese Party which I have cited. When they refused to adhere to the Moscow treaty for a partial test ban, they proposed that a World Disarmament Conference be called with the specific purpose of abolishing nuclear weapons and military bases on foreign soil. (18) Of course we are all opposed to military bases and nuclear weapons and seek the framework in which we can do without them; but the Chinese must be unaware of the susceptibilities of much of the rest of the world if they seriously think that countries would give away just those arms which presumably hold in check the Chinese themselves at a time in their history when they have given some clear evidence of readiness to use their growing conventional military might in their own interests.

Moreover, the Chinese leaders have repeatedly stated that they were doing everything possible to develop nuclear weapons. Marshal Chen Yi, the Peking Foreign Minister, said so on the Swiss Radio network when he came to Geneva in 1962 for the Laos Conference. And a few weeks after proposing a conference to abolish nuclear weapons, he reiterated the Chinese determination to produce nuclear weapons, apparently even if this should mean going without production in other fields. (19)

It is to be hoped that France and China will revise their present attitudes. Meanwhile, it is another token of the intent of the negotiators at Geneva that, while realizing that the absence of France and China create serious difficulties and that sooner or later a strong effort will be necessary to bring these countries into the disarmament effort, they continue, now well into the third year, to negotiate for agreements in the field of arms control and disarmament.

For the best part of two years I sat through the Conference and negotiated as the representative of India. This study is based directly on that participation and my continued close following of the developments at the Geneva Conference.

---

(18) **New York Times,** August 25 1963.

(19) **New York Times,** October 29, 1963.

CHAPTER II

Organization, Procedures and the Delegations

A. *Organization and Procedures*

1. The Co-Chairman of the Conference.—Several of the countries chosen to serve in the 18-Nation Committee had, for the ten months preceding the convening of the disarmament conference, experienced the tactful bridge-building operations of the co-chairmen of the International Conference on the Question of Laos. (This latter Conference was still in session, since final agreement between the three factions in Laos, which alone could bring into effect the international treaty on the neutrality, independence, and territorial integrity of Laos, had not yet been reached.) This success of the presiding function at the Laos Conference was to a great extent due to the adroit handling of their duties by Malcolm Macdonald of the United Kingdom and Georgyi Pushkin (since deceased) of the Soviet Union, who functioned as the heads respectively of the United Kingdom and the Soviet delegations; and, as such, were the co-chairmen of the Conference.

Since the President of the United States and the Chairman of the Council of Ministers of the Soviet Union, the two principal States involved in the arms race and therefore in disarmament, had made several statements indicating their deep interest in disarmament discussions, it seemed likely that they would appoint as heads of their delegations persons who would command the confidence of the Conference. Taking these factors into account before the 18-Nation Disarmament Committee convened, the delegations of Canada and India—two of the non-great power countries which were also represented at the Conference on Laos—proposed that the heads of the delegations of the United States and the Soviet Union should be the co-chairmen of the Disarmament Conference. This matter was quickly settled in private conversations at Geneva when the delegations assembled for the Conference. The very first document of the Conference, No. ENDC/1 of March 14, 1962, states that, "The Permanent Co-Chairmen of the Committee will be the Representatives of the Union of Soviet Socialist Republics and the United States of America . . . The Co-Chairmen will consult with each other and other delegations as desirable with the aim of facilitating both the formal and informal work of the Conference." (20)

This arrangement has undoubtedly worked well. Proof of this is that the co-chairmen have used the dry words of the aforementioned conference

---

(20) ENDC/1, dated March 14, 1964, par. 5.

agreement, which sounds as though their discussions would be purely procedural, to turn many of their two or three meetings a week into probings of substantive matters. Thus, it was at such meetings that the idea of a direct communication link between Washington and Moscow was first mooted, and it was at these meetings, and at technical sessions arranged by the two delegations of the United States and the Soviets, that the details of the direct line agreements were worked out.

Furthermore, from time to time, both co-chairmen tell the heads of other delegations that they have raised a particular matter of substance with each other at their last meeting. Depending on the nature of the matter, and the agreement relating to it among the co-chairmen, we are or are not told the substance of the discussion between the two co-chairmen or are simply appraised of the subject of the discussion. Finally, heads of delegations, particularly of the nonaligned delegations, often use the fact of these co-chairmen meetings to bring to the notice of the two super Powers certain ideas which they might hesitate to expose in conference session.

2. Nature of Meetings.—Taking into account the terms of the General Assembly resolution which mandated the conference, (21) the Committee decided at the very beginning that its meetings should be private, except when otherwise agreed by the participating States. It has never been seriously proposed that the Committee hold public meetings, in spite of the known opposition of the Press to private meetings and also the opposition of numerous groups and individuals (among others Mr. Philip Noel Baker, the British Nobel laureate for peace). However, conventions which have grown up greatly diminished the privacy of the Committee's sessions. To those conventions I refer in the next section of this chapter.

3. Publicity.—It was agreed, also on the very first day, that publicity of the Committee's discussions would be limited to a communique prepared by the chairman of the session. (The routine business of taking the chair at the sessions of the Committee rotates among the heads of delegations on a day to day basis in the alphabetical order of the names of the countries they represent.) But the chairman is not left much discretion as to what should go into the communique. This is what the agreed rule of procedure says: "Normally it (the communique) will refer to the chairmanship of the meeting; the title of any new documents tabled; agreements reached; and, when required, the release of Committee verbatim records and documents." (22) The directions could be hardly more precise.

(21) General Assembly Resolution 1722 (XVI) Part II operative paragraph 2 reads, "Recommends that the Committee, as a matter of the utmost urgency, should undertake negotiations with a view to reaching, on the basis of the Joint Statement of Agreed Principles and taking into account, **inter alia,** paragraph 8 of those Principles, agreement on general and complete disarmament under effective international control;"

(22) ENDC/1, dated March 14, par. 3.

The actual communiques released are even less interesting than the above instructions might suggest. This is mainly because there have been, from day to day, practically no agreements reached and therefore nothing to say on this score; and secondly because the last phrase about the release of documents is not as exciting as it sounds. This matter is governed by another paragraph of the agreed procedural arrangements which says: "Normally verbatim records will be made available after a delay of two weeks for public use through the United Nations Secretariat at Geneva and New York unless otherwise decided." (23) In practice it has taken more like four than two weeks for the documents and verbatims to be distributed by the Secretariat—through no fault of theirs. The process of delegates checking their statements, sending in final versions, and the arrangements to produce the documents in all the four official languages— English, French, Russian and Spanish—has proved to be a more time consuming one than originally anticipated.

But these restrictions on publicity have broken down. It was too much to expect delegates to take the risk of garbled accounts of their statements getting to the Press by "leaks." The result is that, without amending the agreed interdiction, the convention grew of delegates informing the Press of the contents of their own statements. Delegates who speak from written texts make it a practice to hand them to the Press on delivery of these statements.

But this is not all. The convention of releases to the Press has been further amplified. The leading delegations—regularly those of the United States, the Soviet Union and the United Kingdom—hold press briefings after each session to inform the Press not only of the statements of their countries but of all the statements made at the Conference. This has been welcomed by the Press, but at first was resented by those delegations which did not hold regular press briefings. They felt their statements were not being accurately reported. This was inevitably so, and has been largely rectified by the heads of the smaller delegations themselves briefing the Press whenever they have deemed it necessary to do so, especially on statements which they have made.

As a result of the mitigating conventions here referred to, the meetings of the Committee are now private only in name. This should be taken into account by the Conference and should lead to a review of the present rules regarding both publicity and the private character of at least some of its sessions.

4. Informal Meetings.—In the first week or ten days of the life of the Committee there was a strong desire, particularly among the nonaligned

---

(23) ENDC/1, dated March 14, 1964, par. 4.

delegations, to give every possible impetus to the finding of a solution to the problem of the cessation of nuclear weapons testing. At the suggestion of these delegations, two or three informal meetings were held in March 1962 in order to explore various possibilities in this field.

Taking these meetings into account the Committee decided on March 28, 1962, (24) that further informal meetings could be held as appropriate. This provision has been largely a dead letter. I, alone of all delegates, twice called for informal meetings during the years 1962 and 1963. On both occasions such meetings were held, and I used them to direct a series of searching questions to the two sides. The first meeting seemed to be really useful as it did to some extent open up questions such as verification, which had become very difficult. But this technique has its limitations. No records at all are kept of these informal meetings. There is, therefore nothing to go on; nothing to confirm that a particular delegation expressed a particular view. Yet, they have their uses. A delegation which has been drawn out at such a session can usually be persuaded to say something on the same lines in the "private" regular sessions.

In fact, the first indication given by the Soviets that they might move forward in the matter of verification arrangements for agreed disarmament measures in regard to vehicles for the delivery of nuclear weapons was given very tentatively at one of the two informal sessions to which I have referred, and later re-stated at a regular session. Furthermore, at informal meetings the nonaligned have been more sharply incisive in the criticism of the two sides for their lack of movement toward agreements, and have been able, without embarrassing either side on the record, to make suggestions and to urge them forward. Indeed, for this reason alone there should be more of these sessions. I think it is true to say that they have not been actively welcomed by the super Powers. Requests for such sessions have never come from them or from their closest partners in the negotiations.

At the commencement of the 1964 sessions of the Conference, General E.L.M. Burns, the very constructive delegate of Canada, hinted that his delegation would ask for some such meetings. Canada, it might be pointed out, is jokingly referred to at Geneva as the ninth nonaligned country. This is not to say that the Canadians break the unity of the Western Powers in the open meetings, but behind the scenes their urgings are felt and known to be in the direction of possible compromise explorations.

Then again, they have been the quickest among the Western Powers to respond to Soviet moves, as Foreign Minister Howard Green was at the UN General Assembly when Mr. Gromyko proposed in September 1962

---

(24) ENDC/1 Add. 1, dated March 28, 1962.

12

that the nuclear umbrella should remain open on both sides until the end of the Second Stage of disarmament. And when the Conference had before it this proposal, it was again General Burns who did most of the probing of it on the Western side. In doing so he, of course, exposed its weaknesses as well as those aspects of it which might be further considered. Again, in 1963 when Mr. Gromyko proposed that the umbrella remain open until the end of the disarmament plan, Mr. Lester Pearson, the Prime Minister of Canada, was among the first to comment on the new tone of the Soviet contribution to the General Debate in the Assembly. It is interesting that General Burns should have reopened the question of informal sessions for 1964. When the Committee reconvened in February 1964 he was one of the two or three original negotiators still at the table.

5. Direction of Work.—In its procedural decision of the 28th of March 1962 the Conference laid down the directions in which it would attempt to move forward. I have already referred to the third and final paragraph of this document, which relates to the holding of informal meetings.

The first paragraph says that, "in its plenary sessions, the Committee should pursue, without delay, its primary objective of reaching agreement on general and complete disarmament." (25)

The second paragraph states that, "concurrently . . . and not to the detriment of this (the above) elaboration, a committee of the whole . . . (will consider) . . . various proposals on the implementation of measures aimed at: the lessening of international tensions; the consolidation of confidence among states; and facilitating general and complete disarmament." (26)

All these decisions remain in force, and today the Committee meets in two main meetings each week: one devoted to GCD (general and complete disarmament), and the other to collateral measures, (with the kind of objectives laid down in the latter of the paragraphs cited above).

For the first three months or so of its existence one meeting a week was that of a sub-committee of the three nuclear powers of the Committee, at which the sole subject was the reaching of agreements to end nuclear testing. The nonaligned never really favored this arrangement, for the simple reason that we saw in it a continuation of the fruitless debates among the nuclear powers which had been going on since 1958 on the issue of nuclear weapon tests. We made it known to the nuclear powers that all, or some, of us were prepared to be part of the sub-committee on the cessation of nuclear tests. But though there was some sentiment among them in favor of our view they were unable to reach agreement on a sub-committee con-

_____

(25) ENDC/1/Add. 1, dated March 28, 1963.

(26) Ibid.

taining representatives of the non-nuclear powers. Their own arrangement was unsatisfactory and broke down, in essence, long before the Soviets refused to attend further meetings of the three power subcommittee. This breakdown manifested itself in the unanimously agreed arrangement that once a week a meeting of the plenary conference would be devoted entirely to the test ban—which meant that at these plenary sessions the nuclear Three were repeating to us what they said to each other at the meetings of the sub-committee. This year (1964) there are no regular weekly sessions on the subject of the test ban. It will, presumably, be dealt with as one of the collateral measures to be discussed from time to time as agreed.

6. Procedure for Taking Decisions.—There is no provision for taking votes at the Conference. This means that all decisions have to be unanimous. Each of the seventeen States at Geneva in theory exercises a veto power. But it is not this power which causes the lack of substantive progress in disarmament. The reason for the acceptance of the rule of unanimity by the Committee is, first and foremost that it avoids the possibility of either side to the Cold War trying to get its way by mustering votes in the Committee. It is obvious that it would be totally unrealistic to think that the Cold War or any part of it could be brought to an end by a majority decision. If that had been possible the Cold War could have been ended many years ago. Besides, the whole purpose of the Conference is to seek agreements and not partisan victories.

For the nonaligned participants this procedure is of special significance. It is on them that a voting system would bring the odium of any decision: and all decisions which were not unanimous would be odious to one side or the other. The two sides would vote in predictable patterns, placing the nonaligned in the position of judges. They would not accept this position, and nor, indeed, would either of the two sides. The issues of security involved are too basic to be handed over to other parties to decide.

I might add that it would be wrong to suppose that a voting procedure necessarily helps in arriving at decisions which can be implemented. One can point to scores of UN General Assembly decisions, many of them adopted by enormous majorities, which have never been implemented. The most striking series of such UN resolutions are those on South Africa. On the other hand, the Laos Conference, which also proceeded on the basis of unanimous decisions, did work out an international treaty and a protocol which have been implemented at least in part, and the attempt fully to implement them is continuing. It should be remembered that the Laos Conference arrived at its decisions even though at it there was a confrontation between the United States and the Peking Government: prima facie one of the least promising negotiations of our times for the reaching of agreements.

7. The Delegations.—Mr. Khrushchev made a bid for the Geneva conference to begin at the topmost level. In his letters to the Heads of the other 17 Governments or States he said that he did not, of course, expect final agreements to follow from the adoption of his suggestion, but he argued that, "if the result of their efforts is at least to set the negotiations on the right track and to outline the contents of a treaty on general and complete disarmament, that will be a tremendous step forward." (27)

President Kennedy in reply said, ". . . It does mean that much clarifying work will have to be done in the early stages of negotiation before it is possible for Heads of Government to review the situation . . . I do not mean to question the utility or perhaps even the necessity of a meeting of Heads of Government. Indeed, I am quite ready to participate personally at the Heads of Government level at any stage of the Conference when it appears that such participation could possibly affect the chances of success . . ." (28) He went on to recommend that the Conference open at the level of Foreign Ministers, and this is what happened.

The Foreign Ministers stayed only ten days or so. They all expressed hope for the future. Most striking to me were the contributions of the Foreign Ministers of Brazil and Mexico. These countries, particularly Brazil, had not in the United Nations been particularly known for taking "unaligned" positions. But the statements of their Foreign Ministers foreshadowed a staunchly unaligned position at the Conference, and this has, in fact been scrupulously and most helpfully maintained through the two years and more that the Committee of Eighteen has been in being. The following brief quotations, which are representative of the opening statements of the two Foreign Ministers, will serve to give an indication of the consistent approach of these countries:

On March 16, 1962, Foreign Minister de San Thiago Dantas of Brazil said, "We wish to make a contribution to disarmament consistent with the priority we always give to peace in our foreign policy, and we are sure that the best way of doing so is to preserve our independence of judgment and the authority of our voice, in order to lend them to everything calculated to promote effective and immediate disarmament, and to refuse them to everything that merely aggravates polemics, emphasizes antagonisms, impresses public opinion or delays settlements." (29)

In his opening statement for Mexico in March 22, 1962, Foreign Minister M. Tello quoted the following from the letter of President Lopez

---

(27) U.S. Arms Control and Disarmament Agency, **Documents on Disarmament, 1962, Vol. I, p. 35.**

(28) Ibid, p. 37.

(29) ENDC/PV. 3, dated March 16, 1962, p. 7.

Mateos, dated February 22 in reply to Mr. Khrushchev's letter of February 10: "As their (the nonnuclear powers) countries have no immediate interest in the particular formula or formulas by which it is attempted to solve the problem, they are in a good position to play a part of moderation, to seek conciliatory formulas, to serve as a link between the great Powers, and to encourage the representatives of those Powers not to become discouraged, but, bearing in mind the magnitude of the problem, to persevere until a solution is found. Their contribution, and I can assure you that the Mexican delegation will be animated by this spirit, will thus consist in harmonizing the apparently divergent interests of the other Powers in order to ensure that the common desire which unites us all—general and complete disarmament—is not brought to naught by considerations which may be purely adventitious." (30)

France has never come to the 18-Nation Committee. India deplored the absence of France, and in our opening statement we suggested that fresh moves be made to try to persuade the Government of France to send a delegation to the Conference. This led to an informal decision that the then foreign Minister of Italy (Signor A. Segni, now President of Italy) should raise this matter with M. Couve de Murville, the Foreign Minister of France, with whom he was about to meet at Brussels. We later learnt that the matter had been raised but without a positive result at that time. Later, speaking on behalf of India, I again urged the co-chairmen to reopen the matter with the French Government. I understood that this was done once, but there was still no change in the position of the French Government.

After the departure of the Foreign Ministers by the end of the March 1962, the Conference was left to senior negotiators of the 17 Governments in attendance. Throughout the rest of the year 1962 the delegation of the United States was led by Mr. Arthur Dean, thus establishing the continuing importance that the Administration attached to maintaining a high level of negotiation with a view to obtaining results. The Soviets responded by placing at the head of their team Mr. Valerian Zorin, a seasoned Deputy Foreign Minister, and when he was absent his place was taken by an even higher ranking Soviet diplomat, Mr. Vasily Kuznetsov, First Deputy Foreign Minister, whose UN experience goes back to the San Francisco Conference of 1945 at which, on the Soviet side he was number two to Foreign Minister V. Molotov.

The nonaligned too were led by men of relevant experience. Their doyen was Padilla Nervo of Mexico, who had also been present at the 1945 San Francisco conference, and whose involvement with the UN had been almost unbroken since then, including a period when he was Foreign Minister of Mexico. Other senior representatives included the very able

---

(30) **ENDC/PV.** 7, dated March 22, 1962, p. 2.

Mr. Fattah Hassan, a former Deputy Foreign Minister of the United Arab Republic; and Senor de Mello Franco of Brazil, who had been an attachè on the Brazilian delegation at the 1932 League of Nations Disarmament Conference. (He was succeeded at the present Conference by Mr. de Arujo Castro, later Foreign Minister of Brazil.) Nigeria has usually sent Mr. Matthew Mbu, Minister of State for Defense; Ethiopia has had able and senior Ambassadors in charge; and one of the strongest and most valuable delegations has been that of Sweden, generally led by Madame Alva Myrdal, ex-ambassador to India, a member of the Parliament of Sweden and a diplomat of great skill and understanding. The Asian diplomats were James Barrington of Burma, one of the seniormost and best known at the UN of the diplomats of his country, and myself for India—with a continuous involvement with the UN and its agencies since 1951. Most of these nonaligned delegates are no longer at Geneva for the 1964 meetings, the exceptions being Ambassadors Myrdal, Hassan and Barrington. Since the long experience of some of those who have left did not tip the scales on the side of much substantive progress, there is no reason to deplore the changes.

As to the other delegations, I have already referred to the significant contribution being made by Canada, and it is good that this country continues to be represented by Ambassador E.M.L. (Tommy) Burns, who, with his experience as the commander of UN peace-keeping forces, and his general dedication to the cause of disarmament, is a particularly useful delegate. The Communist delegations are competently represented at the level of Deputy Foreign Minister, and I think it would be generally accepted that some helpful contributions have been made, particularly by the delegates of Poland and Rumania, whose Manfred Lachs and George Macavescu respectively have been outstanding delegates; though this is no way meant to denigrate the contributions of other delegates in the group. In general, it is fair to say that while the Communist delegations have stood together with the U.S.S.R., there have at times been slight differences of emphasis in their interventions; and in private conversation these delegates have consistently shown a willingness and an apparent freedom to discuss matters. In such discussions I often felt that I learnt of possible fresh approaches to current issues. I valued my talks with the delegates I have mentioned, and with others, including Tarabanov of Bulgaria and Hajeck of Czechoslovakia.

The British have always been strongly represented by a Minister of State in the Foreign Office—Joseph Godber and then Peter Thomas—backed by a senior Foreign Service Ambassador: Michael Wright and then Paul Mason. There is no doubt that, behind the scenes, the British have been very active at this Conference. In the various moves made in the test ban discussions in particular, their influence was felt. I might mention that at the Conference there has grown up the practice of informal periodic meetings of the four Commonwealth delegations. These meetings serve to acquaint both Nigeria and India with fuller details of the positions of the

Western side, and they give us an opportunity to try out various ideas on the United Kingdom and the Canadian delegations.

The Italians are late comers to the United Nations and to post-war negotiations of this type. Nevertheless, they add their distinctive probings at the negotiating table, ably led by Francesco Cavalletti. The Italians certainly excel, in their group, in the art of hospitality which at such a conference can play an important role and is on the whole not enough exploited by most other delegations.

8. The United Nations Secretariat.—UN General Assembly resolutions are invariably laconic about the role of the UN Secretariat at such conferences. (31) Strictly speaking that role flows from Article 98 of the UN Charter, in terms of which it would amount to a housekeeping and purely administrative task. But Dag Hammarskjold, with his successfully demonstrated new concept of the Security Generalship, established the practice of what he termed the UN presence being available at these forums. He himself was supposed to symbolize that presence, but as he could not be everywhere, his senior officers deputed for him. U. Thant has continued this practice, and during most of 1962 one of his most senior inner cabinet members, Omar Loutfi (who like myself had been Thant's colleague at the United Nations for many years when all of us were Permanent Representatives of our countries) was at Geneva, and his exceptionally sage advice was there for any delegation to seek. After Loutfi's sudden death early in 1963 his place has been taken at times by Under Secretary Dragon Protisch, a very senior UN official. When Protisch cannot be at Geneva, Arvind Vellodi, the very able senior Director in the Division will be there. They are assisted by William Epstein, another very experienced UN officer, and many others. U. Thant himself has only once been able to address the Conference and attend a session, but through the aforementioned galaxy of senior and able men, to whom must be added their ranking member, Under Secretary Suslov, he keeps himself informed and stands ready and prepared to take an initiative in the field of disarmament should the occasion for doing so arise. In view of the still increasing role of the Secretary-General of the United Nations, the presence of the United Nations—in the somewhat mystical sense propounded by Dag Hammarskjold—is a ponderable the effect of which must not be discounted.

---

(31) For its functions at the 18-Nation Conference see G.A. Res. No. 1722 (XVI), dated Dec. 20, 1961, Part II, Para. 4.

CHAPTER III

The Battle of Negotiation Is Joined

As negotiations began, immediate pressure was directed to the question of weapons testing. There was opposition: I have mentioned the rejection of the offer of the nonaligned to assist in the detailed negotiations. In addition, the Soviets and their friends said to us privately that what was needed was to get on with the primary purpose of the conference which, they pointed out, both in terms of the relevant General Assembly resolution and the agreed procedure of work at the Conference, was general and complete disarmament.

In spite of these attitudes the nonaligned pressed for concentration on the test ban. To us this issue was a challenge to the sincerity and determination of the nuclear powers to seek agreements in the general field of arms control and disarmament. On March 21, 1962 Mr. Mahmud Fawzi, the Foreign Minister of the U.A.R. said:

"The world would not forgive us and we should not forgive ourselves if we allowed any more tests under any pretext and for any reason whatsoever to take place again." (32)

Speaking for Mexico, Ambassador Padilla Nervo said on April 3, 1962:

"We do not think that any progress can be made in the negotiations on general and complete disarmament without first discontinuing nuclear explosions and guaranteeing, by means of a contractual obligation and adequate international control, that such tests will never be resumed." (33)

The other six nonaligned representatives spoke in similar vein, but the positions of the two sides seemed unbridgeable. The West asserted that an international control system was necessary to police a ban on tests in all environments—not just in respect of a ban on underground tests. (34) To this the Soviet response was flatly negative. Joseph Godber, the British delegate, asked the Soviet delegate the following question:

---

(32) ENDC/PV. 6, dated March 21, 1962, p. 13.

(33) ENDC/PV. 14, dated April 3, 1962, p. 18.

(34) ENDC/PV. 15, dated April 4, 1962, pp. 13-14, statement of Ambassador Arthur Dean for the U.S.A.

"Does the Soviet Union really offer us no hope of any form of international inspection of any unidentified events in the Soviet Union, in any circumstances, short of the achievement of general and complete disarmament." (35)

The next day Zorin, the Soviet delegate replied: "I shall not beat about the bush. There is no hope." (36)

Thus, there appeared to be no hope at all for negotiations between the two sides on this crucial test issue. This realization had a profound effect on the eight nonaligned delegations. Unlike the two Western and Socialist groupings, we had not come to the conference as a bloc or group. We were eight individual nonaligned delegations, each trying to assess world problems in the light of our backgrounds and experience. Some of the delegates, particularly the Swedes, repeatedly made it explicit that the eight in no sense constituted a bloc. This was so. Nevertheless, the deadlock between the two sides, on the very first practical issue to arise—that of nuclear tests—galvanized the eight into joint action. *Ad hoc* we became a very active and closely knit group.

We met each day, some times more than once. A small drafting committee was set up consisting of the Representatives of Ethiopia, Sweden and India. We prepared the scheme contained in what became the eight power memorandum of April 16, 1962 (37) and submitted it to our remaining colleagues. After long meetings and rapid sequence of them, we got agreement among the eight delegates. This united front and the fact that most of our Foreign Ministers had but two or three weeks previously proclaimed at the same Conference the urgency of the issue and the need to solve it, assisted us in obtaining quickly—fortunately before the two sides could express their doubts at our capital cities about an initiative by us— the sanctions of our home Governments.

Thus was presented a proposal which gave a new impetus to the debate on the banning of tests. First, it reaffirmed the need for an international system of control, based on national systems of seismic posts (to be supplemented as agreed). Secondly, the whole scheme of our proposal, and the provision we made for clearing the nature of dubious events, including the entry of the International Commission into a country, at its invitation, in extreme cases, to examine seismic evidence, made it clear that we had in mind possible violations only through underground tests. Thus, we differed from the then stated Western position by restricting the scope of

---

(35) ENDC/PV. 14, page 35, dated April 3, 1962.

(36) ENDC/PV. 15, page 24, dated April 4, 1962.

(37) ENDC/28, dated April 16, 1962.

controls solely to doubtful *underground* events. In so doing we were, in fact, not going much further than the Kennedy-Macmillan proposal (38) of September 3, 1961, which had proposed to Khrushchev that atmospheric tests be ended without a system of controls. (The offer was not accepted, and it lapsed.) Thirdly, by admitting the need for a certain degree of on-site inspection, to be implemented by an ingenious system of invitations, which an International Commission (preferably nonaligned) would stimulate, we conceded the substance of a basic Western principle.

The wisdom of presenting this proposal was vividly illustrated, both immediately before and after the event, by the attitude of the two super Powers. As I was largely responsible for the contents and the language of the eight power proposal, I followed a style of courtesy upon which I had acted over the years at the United Nations, and decided that before actual presentation of the document at the conference I should show it to both the U.S. and the Soviet delegations. I did so, and both of them reacted with vigorous opposition. This was to be expected. Our proposals would require of both sides changes in their positions. Zorin was particularly vehement in his opposition—our scheme would force him from the position that no on-site inspection would be possible in the Soviet Union except in the context of general and complete disarmament. But the U.S. delegation too made it quite clear that they did not wish the proposal to be presented. However, all the eight governments had by now approved the proposal, and the nature of the objections raised to it by the two sides seemed to me not to warrant its being withheld. The eight nonaligned went on to present the proposal on April 16, 1962.

On the 19th of April 1962 Zorin read into the record a statement by the Soviet Government on our proposals. The statement contained the following phrase:

"For its part, the Soviet Government expresses its willingness to study the proposals set out in the Memorandum of the neutralist States as a basis for further negotiations. " (39)

On April 20, 1962 Arthur Dean speaking for the U.S. said: "We accept it as a basis for discussion, but not as the exclusive basis for discussion." (40)

For the next five months the three nuclear Powers debated this nonaligned memorandum. On the surface this sometimes appeared to be a

---

(38) U.S. Arms Control and Disarmament Agency, **Documents on Disarmament, 1961, p. 351.**

(39) ENDC/PV. 24, dated March 19, 1962, p. 10.

(40) ENDC/PV. 25, dated April 20, 1962, p. 24.

futile operation. On the contrary, it was an intricate, sustained probing, on both sides, of the possibilities of the situation. This was negotiation in its essence: exploration to the limits. It is not the purpose of this study to review that debate, but it would I believe be of value to indicate several significant points that emerged from it.

First, the Soviets realized that the position stated by them at the commencement of the Conference of adamant rejection of on-site inspections in the Soviet Union until there was general and complete disarmament, was one which the nonaligned, who were willing and anxious to understand their position with sympathy, could not support. We never wavered in this conclusion. What is more, I privately urged Zorin and Kuznetsov to make their position more positive on acceptance of the eight power memorandum by stating clearly that they would, in fact, invite the International Commission to visit certain scenes of doubtful events, and that they would submit themselves to a degree of on-site inspection. I believe we got some satisfaction of these urgings, and thereby shifted, at least in some degree, the basic premises governing the very difficult but crucial issue of verification in the whole field of arms control and disarmament. Thus, on May 9, 1962 Zorin said:

"We made a move to meet the proposals put forward by the Eight Powers. We adopted this new position in regard to inspection, because previously we spoke of rejecting any inspection whatsoever, but now we say this inspection is admissible on a voluntary basis . . . we agree that it will be possible in individual cases to invite scientists, members of the International Commission, to ascertain *in loco* the nature of the events which are in doubt. (41)

Kuznetsov's statement in August 1962 was even more forthcoming, (42) and on August 15, 1962, Manfred Lachs, speaking for Poland said:

"What more can the Soviet Union have done? The memorandum speaks of invitation. The Soviet Union says, "We shall invite." (43)

These were important statements. They remain on the record. There can be little doubt that the scheme of the eight Nation memorandum, which was the sole basis of negotiation for a test ban to be endorsed by the Seventeenth session of the UN General Assembly, (44) was one of the factors which prompted the Soviets, immediately after the General Assembly

---

(41) ENDC/PV. 35, dated May 9, 1962, pp. 48-49.

(42) ENDC/PV. 71, pp. 42-43.

(43) ENDC/PV. 70, p. 13.

(44) G.A. Res. 1762 (XVII), Part A, par. 4, dated Nov. 6, 1962.

session, to write to the President of the United States proposing a test ban on the basis of two or three on-site inspections a year. This offer was tangible evidence of some movement away from the complete rejection by the Soviet Government of inspection on Soviet territory except as part of an agreed treaty on general and complete disarmament, and even then not until actual disarmament was reaching its final phases. The Eight Nation memorandum certainly would appear to have played no small part in stimulating this most significant shift.

Secondly, by refusing, at any point to agree with the West that the international control system should be capable of monitoring a weapons test prohibition in all four environments (atmosphere, outer space, under water and under ground) the Eight at Geneva must surely have played a part in getting the United States and the United Kingdom to do some rethinking on the minimum necessary scope of an international control system. The outcome was their proposing, on August 27, 1962, two draft treaties for a test ban: one a comprehensive treaty (45) in which there would be on-site inspections in respect only of doubtful underground events and the other a draft treaty to stop tests in the other three environments without any international control. (46) The Eight Nation effort helped in opening the door to a firm Western position on a ban without controls in all but one environment. The firming up of this position was one of the foundations of the partial test ban when it finally came on July 25, 1963.

Thirdly, the weight of the Eight Nation memorandum both at the Geneva discussion and at the succeeding session of the General Assembly of the UN at which it was overwhelmingly endorsed (though the two super Powers abstained on resolution 1762 XVII as a whole they voted for the endorsement of the Eight Nation memorandum) increased the standing of the nonaligned at the Geneva Conference as partners in negotiation. The nonaligned, of course, entirely concede the primacy of interest of the nuclear powers in the matter of arms control and disarmament, but they do not at all accept President de Gaulle's view that negotiations should involve nuclear powers alone.

The Eight Power memorandum reminded the two sides to the Cold War that if they ran out of ideas on crucial aspects of the work of the Conference there would be others who would make suggestions, and do so perhaps with the endorsement of the General Assembly. This fact makes disarmament negotiations much less brittle than they were when they were confined to the two sides.

The highlights in the year 1962 in regard to the test ban were (a) the Eight Nation memorandum of April 16, (b) the U.S.-U.K. draft treaties

---

(45) ENDC/58, dated Aug. 27, 1962.

(46) ENDC/59, dated Aug. 27, 1962.

of August 27, 1962, (c) the endorsement by the General Assembly on November 6, of the Eight Nation memorandum, (d) Mr. Khrushchev's letter to President Kennedy of December 19 (47) proposing negotiations for a comprehensive test ban on the basis of two or three inspections per year in the territories of each nuclear power, and Mr. Kennedy's reply of December 28. (48)

The failure of the New York talks on the basis of the Kennedy-Khrushchev correspondence of December 1962 sent Geneva off on a new tack, ignoring the General Assembly's endorsement of the Eight Nation memorandum. This was the period of the numbers game—should there be ten, seven, six, five or less inspections per year in order to give each side enough sense of security against possible violations by the other side? In February 1963 the United States specifically brought down its demand from twelve per year to seven. (49) Furthermore, subsequent to that, on March 1, 1963 William Foster at the conference stated: "We have been attempting on our part to conduct real negotiations on this number of on-site inspections. In sum, we want to negotiate . . . the relationship between the quota number and the inspections arrangements has been clearly recognized. . . ." (50) This gave us all to understand that the U.S. figure could perhaps go down still further. On the other hand, the Soviets maintained that in private the delegates and scientists of the United States had assured them that no more than two or three inspections per year were necessary. Besides, Kuznetsov and Tsarapkin would assert this was the U.S. position, whereas that of the Soviet's was that no inspections were necessary. (51) In agreeing to two or three inspections Tsarapkin claimed the Soviets were accepting the U.S. position so as to enable the administration to get the U.S. Senate to agree to a test ban. To the nonaligned it seemed inconceivable that a test ban should hang simply on the question as to whether there should be X or Y inspections per year when the difference between X and Y was no more than the figure 3, or at most 4.

At the conference all of us said this, and in private we expressed ourselves more strongly to the two super Powers, but the tantalizing gap remained. In this situation the eight nonaligned decided that again it was their duty to act together and to place a compromise proposal before the two sides. Again there were numerous meetings and drafts. Again the eight delegates at Geneva reached agreement among themselves as to the course to be followed. The crucial clause concerned the number of inspec-

(47) ENDC/73, dated January 31, 1963.

(48) ENDC/74, dated January 31, 1963.

(49) ENDC/PV. 102, dated 25 February 1963, p. 24.

(50) ENDC/PV. 104, dated March 1, 1963, pp. 16 and 19.

(51) ENDC/PV. 101, dated February 22, 1963, pp. 26 and 34.

tions per year necessary to deter violation of a treaty to ban all tests. We took scientific advice which seemed to show that from four to five inspections per year, properly spaced over the twelve months, should suffice to assure either side that its opponent or opponents were not indulging in a series of under ground weapons tests (it was agreed on all sides that a violator would need to set off a series of test explosions and not just one or two.) (A scientist attached to one of the nonaligned delegations proved mathematically that the mean between seven and three inspections a year was not five but four decimal five!)

The eight representatives were clear that this issue could not be decided on purely scientific data, especially when the data were susceptible to being interpreted in several different ways. Next we took a still more important decision. This was not to prescribe one magic figure and say that it alone could solve the dispute, but rather further to narrow the range of contention between the two sides. We argued that if we did this we could create a situation in which continued disagreement between the two sides would be nothing short of ridiculous. At the same time, by leaving both sides the possibility of some further negotiation we would salutarily leave to them the last step toward agreement; and by so doing would make it *their* agreement. These, in short, were our views as to the most appropriate negotiating tactics, taking into account the parties to the confrontation and the delicacy and importance of the issue.

Our suggestion was that agreement should be postulated on the basis of the number of inspections being fixed not for one year but for a period of five or seven years. Assuming a period of seven years, we suggested that the number of inspections should be between thirty-one and thirty-five. It would probably be necessary to fix the maximum number of inspections per year to ensure that the seven year quota was not too heavily drawn upon in any one year.

Our proposal was ready. It was before our eight governments for their consideration. But one crucial error had been committed. This time the two sides had become informed of the details of the plan before we were able to obtain the approval of our governments. They knew this was the situation. They made strong and undoubtedly sincere representations to several of the eight governments against the nonaligned plan. Both claimed they would be very seriously embarrassed by it. It is, of course, not the intention of responsible nonaligned governments to embarrass the super Powers in their search for a solution, and both of them assured us that the search was very real and at such a delicate stage that outside efforts would not help. Some of our capitals accepted their *demarches*. The second Eight Nation plan remained stillborn.

As it turned out, it was a profound mistake not to have presented the plan. Our governments withheld it because they understood that the two sides were anxious to reach their own unfettered comprehensive test ban agreement and that they were likely to do so. This did not happen; and when the two sides were approaching the point of failure there was no alternative, official, public, proposal which they were obliged to consider. The Soviets backed away from any quota of on-site inspections and we eventually got not a full test ban but only a partial one.

This failure to present a plan, which occurred in April 1963, stultified the nonaligned at the Conference for the next four months. Indeed, several of the senior nonaligned delegates absented themselves from the Conference for several weeks, and two or three decided that there was little use in continuing to negotiate. To confuse the issue still further, there were private indications to us from the Western side that, after all, it would not have been too bad if we had presented the plan. But when these indications came it was too late to act. The Soviets had made it clear they were no longer prepared to accept on-site inspections.

While it is of course true that the fate of the comprehensive test ban negotiations did not depend solely on the question of numbers of on-site inspections—though this was a very important issue—to the professional negotiator it will remain a catastrophic pity that this issue was not explored to its limits. There was a real and most unfortunate failure of negotiating capacity at the juncture when the Eight decided not to present their plan. At the very least it would have made it very difficult for either side to get away from the effort to reach a comprehensive ban till they had shown that they had studied the nonaligned plan and found it wanting. It is more than probable that the plan, after presentation, would have called for favorable comment both governmental and scientific, thus making it all the more difficult for the two sides to back away from it. For example, the Canadian Government would probably have reacted favorably. The British Government might have had second thoughts about it, and our experience is that the Soviets do not enjoy being in opposition to the whole of the noncommitted world unless their vital interests are involved. In this case, when they had themselves agreed to up to three inspections a year, it cannot be claimed that their vital interests would have been seriously jeopardized by a plan which would have slightly raised the annual figure to an average of four and a fraction.

The failure on the part of the nonaligned to fulfill their duty in the spring of 1963 by presenting their plan for a comprehensive test ban agreement possibly cost us all a full test ban—instead of which we got the partial one negotiated in the latter half of July that year.

There has been a great deal of press speculation as to why the Soviets backed away from their willingness to accept a small number of on-site inspections, and why they seemed finally to prefer a partial test ban to the comprehensive one on which they had hitherto insisted. What was the role of Soviet relations with China, their agricultural shortages, etc.? These are some of the matters which have been debated. I do not consider myself competent to assign precise weights, if any at all, to these factors.

However, I am in a position to say that talks with the representatives of all the Socialist delegations at the Disarmament Conference led me to think that the most important factors were those relating more directly to the negotiations at Geneva. There were questions such as these:

If the Soviets should go up to four or even five inspections a year would the United States come down to these figures or would they hold out for seven? To go up to the latter would look like entirely giving into the United States and this would definitely embarrass the U.S.S.R. both at home and with its group.

Could the United States, indeed, come down at all in the number of inspections and get the treaty through the Senate? Should they try and fail it would, in the Socialist camp, vindicate the position of those elements and Communist parties which hold that it is not possible to come to any agreements with the United States.

If a tentatively acceptable figure of annual inspections could be found by the two sides, what would be the nature of an inspection? Would it mean the intensive survey of an area of about 500 square kilometers?

It seemed that problems such as these might prove to be unsoluble, and if this were so the net result would simply be to strengthen the position of those who argue in the Communist world against the attempt at co-existence with the "Capitalist" world. I was told that it was important for Khrushchev to reach an agreement with the West because he had been proclaiming that this was not only possible but would be all to the good, whereas the Chinese and other opponents had been saying that his idea of agreements was simply unworkable. In these circumstances he settled for what seemed the most practicable at the time.

Assuming that there might be an element of verity in the above analysis, I contend that the Geneva Conference failed in its proper functions in the spring and early summer of 1963 by not fully exploring the other practical possibilities. The Eight, in particular, should certainly have done more than they did to explore the sort of questions I have just mentioned. Perhaps satisfactory answers could have been found, perhaps not. One only knows that when one could have found out, not enough effort was made to do so. It was not sufficient that the two sides knew of the contents of our plan. Not only did the two sides possess this knowledge, but on May 9,

1963 Madame Alva Myrdal, the delegate of Sweden to the Geneva Conference, speaking at the Tenth General Assembly of the World Veterans Federation at Copenhagen, made a public disclosure, with slight alternations, of the details of the plan. (52) What was appropriate to the negotiating needs of the moment was a governmental tabling of the plan so that governmental consideration of it should result. This, in spite of Madame Myrdal's brave effort, we failed to achieve.

(52) **Disarmament is Possible,** (A World Veterans Federation Report), May 1963, pp. 49-50.

CHAPTER IV

The Conference and the Core Problems of Disarmament

A. *The Problems*

The core problems of disarmament may be grouped under six heads:

1. Nuclear and other weapons of mass destruction
2. Delivery systems for nuclear weapons
3. Verification and control of disarmament measures
4. Conventional arms and armed forces
5. Peace keeping machinery and the settlement of disputes
6. Collateral measures or *ad hoc* partial measures in the field of disarmament or arms control

The purpose of this section is to examine and analyze the major attitudes so far expressed at the Geneva Conference toward these core problems, bearing in mind that not all of the problems have been equally discussed, and that none has yet been fully considered, though the Conference is now in its third year. It is desirable to look first at certain factors which help to explain convergence on these core problems, and at certain other factors which determine the nature of the consideration given to them at Geneva.

B. *Factors that Impinge on the Core Problems*

The most important of these factors is that for the first time in the period since World War II there is, and it constitutes now the over-all mandate to be fulfilled by the Geneva Conference, a precise and clear-cut goal in regard to disarmament and arms control. In the past there were vague formulations of the need for comprehensive regulation of armaments (53) and there have been some specific statements in General Assembly resolutions picking out certain aspects of the armament situation for treatment through negotiation (54) (which did not result!), but there was never a precise and agreed over-all goal for disarmament. This was finally achieved in General Assembly resolution number 1722 (XVI) dated December 20, 1961 which *inter alia* reads, "*Recommends* that the Com-

---

(53) G.A. Res. 715 (VIII), dated Nov. 28, 1953.

(54) G.A. Res. 1148 (XII), dated Nov. 14, 1957.

mittee, as a matter of the utmost urgency, should undertake negotiations with a view to reaching—agreement on general and complete disarmament under effective international control." This resolution was introduced jointly by the United States and the U.S.S.R. and was adopted unanimously.

Thus, we met at Geneva on March 14, 1962 with a precise and definite goal. There were, to be sure, murmurs and private doubts among the delegates—one or two had had personal experience of the frustration of inter-war disarmament conferences, and some of us had had ten years or so of similar experience of UN negotiations. All doubts were set at rest by Secretary of State Dean Rusk's explicit confirmation on March 27, 1962 to the Conference, of the goal of the negotiations: "The United States and the Soviet Union are agreed that we should achieve general and complete disarmament. The first part of paragraph 1 of the Joint Statement of Agreed Principles so states. The objective, therefore, is to reduce national armaments to nothing—to zero per cent. This is in the Soviet plan; it is in the United States plan. . . ." (55)

The two super Powers, in the summer of 1961, the recommencement of Soviet nuclear testing notwithstanding, gave a remarkable impetus to disarmament by working out a Joint Statement of Agreed Principles for Disarmament Negotiations. (56) Apart from prescribing the outlines of the provisions of a disarmament treaty, stating the need to proceed in stages to the goal of complete disarmament, and calling for the preservation of the military balance so that no State would in the process of disarmament be put in a position of advantage, the Joint Statement of Agreed Principles virtually laid down a four point goal—for the bald plain goal of a world without arms was obviously too singular to meet the exacting and manifold requirements of the security of men and nations. The four point goal was: (a) "general and complete disarmament." (b) "strict and effective international control as would provide firm assurance that all parties are honoring their obligations." (c) "reliable procedures for the peaceful settlement of disputes" . . . and (d) "effective arrangements for the maintenance of the peace," "including the obligation of States to place at the disposal of the United Nations agreed man power necessary for an international peace force to be equipped with agreed types of armaments." (56)

This agreement on principles put the Geneva Conference at its very start far ahead of any body which had ever sat down to negotiate disarmament. Any study of the Geneva Conference must proceed on the premise that the reader has a thorough knowledge of the contents of the Joint Statement

---

(55) ENDC/PV. 10, dated March 27, 1962, p. 11.

(56) ENDC/5, dated March 17, 1962, (aho UN Document A/4879, dated Sept. 20, 1961).

of Agreed Principles for Disarmament Negotiations; to facilitate this it is printed as an Annex to this study.

In the preamble to the Agreed Principles the super Powers call "upon other States to cooperate in reaching early agreement on general and complete disarmament in a peaceful world in accordance with these principles." This recognition of the role of other States was another new element in the situation. It is this element which led to agreement between the United States and the Soviet Union on eight names of nonaligned States for inclusion in the negotiating forum. Indeed, in terms of the realism of this part of the Joint Principles, it became possible to resolve satisfactorily the long standing problem, which had plagued the scene throughout the post-war period, of finding an appropriate negotiating body. Experience seems to show that this is at last so: the 18-Nation Conference has already had a longer active and more useful life than any previous disarmament negotiating body. This factor of an agreed and composite negotiating body has an important effect on the negotiations. It makes it much more difficult for either side to withdraw from the effort. There is an element of truth in the statement that the two sides are held captive to the table by their political need or desire to vie with each other for the support of the nonaligned eight, who are numerically the largest of the three sections at the Conference.

The first three factors noted—the precise goal, the Joint Principles and the agreed presence of the nonaligned—are all positive in their effect on the work of the Conference. There is, however, a fourth factor to note which is negative. This is the non-cooperation of France, and with this might be mentioned the absence of China. These two dissociations detract from the value of the negotiation. This is widely recognized, and it will soon be a matter of finding the best ways to remedy the situation. Meanwhile, meaningful discussion and tentative agreements in the field of disarmament are possible. It must be remembered that though the Committee may be used by two or more States as a forum for reaching agreements, (the direct communications link (57) between the Governments of the United States and the Soviet Union was negotiated at Geneva between the delegations concerned and signed on behalf of the two Governments by the acting leaders of their delegations on June 20, 1963) the Conference in general can only make agreed recommendations (58) to the Governments of the world. Its work could only become effective after a world conference on disarmament had accepted its recommendations and the process of ratification by Governments had been completed.

---

(57) U.S. Arms Control and Disarmament Agency, **Third General Report, Appendix III.**

(58) G.A. Res. 1722 (XVI), Part II, par. 3.

A fifth and most complex factor remains to be noted. This is the general world climate in which the discussions of the Conference take place. In a real sense there has been a definite growth in sophistication. It is now well recognized that disarmament negotiations cannot wait till the major problems on the international scene have been solved. Both sides have asserted this, and the fact that the disarmament meetings have gone on despite the Cuban crisis, the worsening of the situation in Southeast Asia, the unabated problem of Berlin and Germany, and the upsurge of new tensions on the border of India which, because they concern China, India and Pakistan, involve half of the world's population and potentially a still larger fraction, would seem to show that this assertion is in accordance with the facts. But in detail the degree of sophistication is not sufficient to insulate entirely the Conference from the facts of the world situation. The Soviets and their friends have frequently stated that the moves to strengthen NATO by developing a multilateral nuclear force impede the work of the Conference. This might be a controlled impeding, one that is deployed so as to put pressure on the West to reconsider a policy within its alliance which is certainly not popular with the Warsaw countries. On the whole I would say that the murkiness or otherwise of the international weather does not play a decisive role at the Geneva Conference. On balance it is realized that serious consideration of disarmament must proceed, because inherent in the arms race and in the present armaments situation there are factors which compel such consideration.

C. *The Core Problems*

Considering the generally favorable effect of the impinging factors, and particularly of the agreed directions contained in the Joint Principles, one would be entitled to expect that it might have been possible fairly quickly to come to agreement on some, at least, of the core problems of disarmament. But it turned out that, basing themselves on the Joint Principles, the United States and the U.S.S.R. had two significantly *different* concepts of disarmament which they set out, in the U.S. Outline of Basic Provisions for GCD in a Peaceful World, (59) and the Soviet draft treaty on GCD under strict International Control. (60)

The U.S. concept was to proceed to the "zero point," as Mr. Rusk had termed it, by applying to the present armaments mixes of the two sides across the board percentage cuts gradually reducing armaments to the finally agreeable levels. Broadly speaking, the U.S. plan proceeds at the rate of a ten per cent cut per annum—this is the precise figure for the First Stage of the proposed plan. This stage is to take three years to complete and is to result in a thirty per cent reduction of armaments. Ambassador

---

(59) ENDC/30, dated April 18, 1962.

(60) ENDC/2, dated March 15, 1962.

Arthur Dean, the first U.S. negotiator, explained and defended this philosophy as follows: "My delegation is firmly convinced, however, that we must not disturb the existing military pattern while we are carrying out the process of abolition. I do not say that we must live with this existing degree of acute reciprocal danger, because it is the very aim of our disarmament program to reduce this danger progressively, dramatically and drastically as we proceed from stage to stage. Nevertheless, it is wholly unrealistic to think that the disarmament process itself can be a vehicle for altering the nature of the world military picture, even for the relatively short period during which we are implementing a disarmament treaty."(61)

The same day (May 11, 1962) Valerian Zorin stated the Soviet approach: "What matters is . . . a bold and responsible political decision by their Governments to set about at last the implementation of radical and drastic disarmament measures in the First Stage in order to remove first and foremost the tremendous threat of a nuclear missile war and thereby clear the way to a thorough disarmament process moving rapidly and right to the end . . ." (62)

In replying to questions by the Swedish representative and myself on the question of balance the late Charles Stelle said for the United States, regarding the principle as set out by Arthur Dean:

"This, we believe, is not an extension of or derivation from the agreed principle of balanced reductions, but merely an attempt to spell it out in different words, in terms of what we believe is the most workable way of implementing the principle. We believe that the additional complexities of trying to negotiate composition, as well as level, of forces and armaments remaining at each stage would only delay and complicate our efforts."(63)

Valerian Zorin defended the Soviet plan's balance as follows: "Where the First Stage of disarmament is concerned, this principle (of balance) is specifically reflected in the fact that our proposal for the complete elimination of the means of delivery of nuclear weapons is linked up with the dismantling of foreign bases on alien territory and with a major reduction of armed forces and so-called conventional armaments . . . if only the means of delivery are eliminated, States having bases on foreign territories will gain certain military advantages. Therefore, in order to exclude such advantage and to preserve the balance between both sides, it is necessary to eliminate foreign military bases in alien territories. As we know, however, attempts are made to justify the existence of foreign military bases

---

(61) ENDC/PV. 35, dated May 11, 1962, p. 7.

(62) ENDC/PV. 35, dated May 11, 1962, p. 62.

(63) ENDC/PV. 37, dated May 15, 1962, p. 7.

by reference to the alleged superiority of the Soviet Union in armed forces and conventional armaments. While we consider such assertions groundless, they are nevertheless made. Therefore, in order to give the other side a sense of confidence, we propose that armed forces should be drastically reduced to a level which would allay any apprehensions of the other side." (64)

Thus, the two sides stoutly defended, in terms of the same principle of balance enjoined by the Joint Principles, two quite different schemes of disarmament.

What was the view of the nonaligned? We conceded that on the face of it the U.S. view was probably in accordance with the principle of balance, but we did not think that that scheme alone, and none other, could meet the requirements of the agreed principle. In order to satisfy the criterion of balance laid down in the Joint Principles, measures of disarmament "should be balanced so that at no stage of the implementation of the treaty could any State or group of States gain military advantage and that security is insured equally for all." 65) It could even be argued that percentage cuts would work out to the advantage of those States which were very strong in a particular sector of armament. Suppose, for example, China would say that it could agree to a disarmament plan only on the basis of percentage cuts, and supposing further that her armed forces now amounted to twelve millions. It is obvious that as percentage cuts continued across the board and other States reduced their more decisive weapons, China would, at the end of say a 65 per cent cut, still have an enormous standing army which could tilt the balance in her favor. In view of this sort of possibility the U.S. plan prescribes a ceiling on force levels. It states in paragraph I of Section B of the Outline for Stage I that the force levels for specified countries other than the United States and the Soviet Union would be reduced to figures not to exceed the force levels prescribed for these two Powers, viz., 2.1 million men. But the Outline does not make the same provision in regard to the thirty per cent cut it prescribes in the First Stage for armaments; and it can be strongly argued that if China (for example) were to keep, at the end of Stage I, 65 per cent of the armaments required for a force of 12 million men she would be placed in a position of very real advantage over most other countries. Thus, it can be shown that even the method of percentage cuts does not necessarily satisfy the criteria of balance as laid down in the Joint Principles.

These and other considerations I pointed out to the United States and other delegates informally. In the Conference I said (in a statement

(64) ENDC/PV. 36, dated May 14, 1962, pp. 34-35.

(65) ENDC/5, dated March 19, 1962, par. 5. See Annex.

delivered before that of Mr. Zorin which I have just quoted) : "While I do not in principle disagree with the United States representative that the pattern may bear some correlation to the balance, it is not precisely what we are asked to do. We are not asked to preserve a pattern of armament. In fact, if we were asked to do so, it might be argued later—and that is another reason why this point is of great importance—that when we had disarmed fully we should still preserve in our national militia and so on the same pattern of armament, namely nuclear weapons and other weapons of mass destruction." (66)

It could probably be accepted that a plan of disarmament which operates on the basis of across the board cuts would in general satisfy the criterion of balance, provided that adjustments were made in regard to the cuts for various categories of weapons. While this is so, I believe that the main reason why, eventually, the agreed plan would have to work on the basis of across the board cuts, perhaps deeper in certain armament categories than in others, is that the United States has built up an armaments mix which she regards as necessary for the preservation of her security and the security of her allies, and that it is not practicable to expect her to abandon that mix till a disarmament plan is well down the road of implementation and until there exist acceptable methods of supplementing national security through international action. This practical and forceful reason outweighs theoretical considerations of perfect balance, and it could be operated in a manner which would not do great violence to that principle. Wheather it is feasible to work out a system which would ensure that the cut being made in a given category of arms actually corresponds to the agreed percentage to be reduced, is yet another question, and one on which most delegations have serious doubts.

Thus in spite of the agreed Joint Principles and the agreed goal, the two sides have very different ideas of how to cut through the existing mazes of arms to the final goal. When the two plans were tabled in March (67) and April (68) 1962 the Conference found itself nowhere near agreement on any of the crucial arms issues or core problems. We can now look at the most significant of those problems in some detail.

1. *Nuclear and other Weapons of Mass Destruction.*—As regards nuclear warheads of various kinds the U.S. plan departs from its norm of percentage across the board cuts. In the First Stage the 30 per cent cut, applied to most other weapons, does not extend to these weapons. The reason for this departure is implied in one of the first stage measures proposed by the United States. It is:

---

(66) ENDC/PV. 36, dated May 16, 1962, p. 28.

(67) The Soviet Plan was tabled as Document ENDC/2, dated March 19, 1962.

(68) The U.S. Plan was tabled as Document ENDC/30, dated April 18, 1962.

"The Parties to the Treaty would agree to examine remaining unresolved questions relating to the means of accomplishing in Stages II and III the reduction and eventual elimination of nuclear weapons stockpiles. In the light of this examination the Parties to the Treaty would agree to arrangements concerning nuclear weapons stockpiles." (69)

The Soviets attacked this formulation strongly, as establishing that the United States had not come to the Conference determined to get rid of nuclear weapons, but to introduce a technical examination of the matter which could easily be so handled as to show that it was not possible to locate or verify the presence of nuclear warheads. Therefore no abolition of nuclear weapons would result under the U.S. scheme. This view was, of course, totally rejected by the U.S. representatives.

The above fundamental difference apart, there are other differences in the approaches of the two sides to the elimination of nuclear weapons. The United States proposes that during the First Stage there should be a verified cessation of the production of fissionable materials for nuclear weapons, and the transfer of agreed quantities of weapons grade U-235 from past production to peaceful uses. In this connection the transfer of 50,000 kilograms each by the United States and the Soviet Union has been mentioned illustratively by the United States. (70) The United States also proposes, and this is its third specific suggestion for nuclear measures in the First Stage of disarmament, that the transfer of fissionable material between States should be under agreed safeguards to be worked out with the International Atomic Energy Agency. The fourth U.S. proposal is agreement on non-dissemination of nuclear weapons, and the fifth is a test ban.

Among the above, two major proposals are the cut-off of production of fissile materials for weapons purposes, and the transfer to peaceful purposes of agreed and significant quantities of such materials. These are some of the United States' earliest and most cherished proposals in the nuclear field. Mr. Stassen pressed them strongly in 1956-57 when he was disarmament negotiator for the United States, and he asked me then why the Soviets flatly rejected them. I suggested that since the Soviets knew the United States to have much larger stocks, both of nuclear weapons and of fissile materials, they were bound to regard these proposals as clearly disadvantageous to themselves. However, the United States and its allies introduced the proposals into their resolution on dis-

---

(69) ENDC/30, Stage I, Part C, par. 6.

(70) ENDC/PV. 31, dated May 4, 1962, p. 19. The United States has also mentioned the transfer by itself of 60,000 kilograms against a transfer of 40,000 kilograms by the U.S.S.R. See ENDC/PV. 166, dated February 13, 1964, p. 32.

armament which the United Nations General Assembly adopted on November 14, 1957. (71)

At the Geneva Conference Mr. Zorin's reply on these proposals was: "I should like to conclude by touching on a question relating to nuclear weapons in connection with the first stage of disarmament. At the meeting of 29 March, Mr. Dean posed the question:

> 'I would like to ask our Soviet colleague why their treaty is so drafted as not to provide that measures for stopping the production of fissionable materials for weapon purposes should be included in Stage I?' (ENDC/PV. 11, p. 11.)

"Mr. Dean showed his lack of understanding. But this lack of understanding surprises us, because Mr. Dean knows perfectlly well the answer to that question. Here is what he himself said a little later, at our meeting of 24 April, on the cessation of production of fissionable materials:

> 'If the measure is one in which the parties agree to halt or limit production, the International Disarmament Organization must have access to the relevant production facilities and activities wherever located.' (ENDC/PV. 26, page 6.)

"This, in plain language, means the establishment of control over the atomic industry. But is this realistic, if at the same time there is no prohibition of nuclear weapons and no measures are carried out to eliminate and destroy them? Every sensible person knows that this is unrealistic. If the United States agrees to prohibit and eliminate nuclear weapons in the First Stage then the conditions will be created for the cessation of production of fissionable materials for military purposes. But the Western Powers have invariably refused, and refuse even now, to agree to such a measure. In these circumstances the cessation of production of fissionable materials for military purposes boils down to yet another form of control without disarmament, or control over armaments. To that of course we cannot agree." (72)

Mr. Zorin was undoubtedly correctly stating the position of his government when he said that the Soviets would not agree to extensive controls without a simultaneous destruction of nuclear weaponry and industry on both sides. But perhaps the basic reason for Soviet opposition remains that the relative situations have not shifted in the seven years since 1957. The Soviets are still well behind in the amount of fissile materials of weapons strength and in stocks of warheads. Indeed, informally I was frequently

---

(71) G.A. Res. No. 1148 (XII), pars. 1 (b) and (c).

(72) ENDC/PV. 29, dated May 2, 1962, pp. 46-47.

told by Western Delegates at the Conference that in terms of megatonage of such weapons the ratio between the United States and the Soviet Union was 10 or 8 to 1. Probably the ratio for back-up stocks of fissile materials is even more favorable to the United States. If it were otherwise I imagine the U.S.S.R. would not only agree to the transfer to peaceful purposes of the suggested 50,000 kilograms of U-235, but perhaps even suggest higher figures. Certainly such a gesture would be of value to them in the nonaligned world. I can only surmise that they are not in a position to make it.

But there is a new force pushing both sides in the direction of agreement on the cut-off of production of fissile materials for weapons purposes. There is mutual agreement, in principle, that as many restrictions as possible should be placed on the emergence of new members of the Atomic Club. An effective check on increases in membership would be an agreement among the present Atomic Powers to cease production of fissile materials for weapons. If they can achieve this, they can then go on to mount a valid and weighty pressure for effective world-wide controls to ensure that there would be no diversion of fissile materials, by any State, to weapons manufacture. Even if France and China refuse to join in such an arrangement, the other nuclear Powers would still have a strong case for insisting on controls on fissile materials produced by other countries.

However, there are countries eager to develop their weapons systems which expect assistance from France or will expect assistance from China. These two leakages in the proposed system of checks could render the system impracticable. Here, as in many other disarmament and arms control issues, we see again the need for action to be truly universal and multilateral. So far as the Geneva discussions are concerned, non-proliferation is at least solidly on the agenda now. On some of the more peripheral First Stage nuclear measures there is agreement, at least in principle. Both plans include First Stage measures against the non-dissemination of nuclear weapons and for a test ban. The remaining issue is the transfer of fissionable materials to other countries under international safeguards. On this point, the Soviet Union, after years of holding a different position—which was backed by many of the non-nuclear powers—has, at the International Atomic Energy Agency recently (1963), come around to accept the view that transfers of nuclear materials to other countries should be under adequate safeguards.

In the Second Disarmament Stage the two plans diverge even more widely with respect to nuclear disarmament. The Soviet plan calls for the complete elimination of all nuclear weapons, the destruction or conversion of all stockpiles to peaceful purposes, the shutting down or conversion, under the supervision of the inspectors of the International Disarmament Organization, of all plants, etc., and control over the extraction of raw materials for the atomic industry. (73) The American plan, on the other hand, proceeds on the basis of its general method of gradualness and proposes that in the light of the technical examination referred to in the First Stage the parties to the treaty agree to make full declaration of the amounts, types, and nature of utilization of all their fissionable materials; reduce, in accordance with agreed percentages, the amounts of such materials used in weapons; destroy the non-nuclear components etc. of weapons from which the fissionable materials have been removed; and accept limitations on the production or refabrication of nuclear weapons from any remaining fissionable materials. (74)

In general the attitude of the nonaligned to the elimination of weapons of mass destruction was to give this aspect of the plans a push forward. Their general feeling was that the main purpose of disarmament must be to remove the nuclear menace. This is understandable. Had not Mr. James F. Byrnes, when discussing the need to control atomic energy, stated: "It is easy to see now what folly it would have been, when gun powder was discovered, to start disarming by limiting the use of the bow and arrow." (75)

Many of the nonaligned suggested that the nuclear menace should be brought under full control by the end of the Second Stage of disarmament. As it turned out, this view was a little naive. It is not in accordance with reality that as long as there is the danger of the use of massive force by States to settle their disputes, those powers which possess decisive weapons should give them up. Only when the whole process of universal disarmament brings the possibility of a massive use of all kinds of force under control, assuming this to be possible, can decisive weapons be given up.

Even the Soviets, though their delegation strove hard at Geneva to gain acceptance of the view that the nuclear menace must be ended in the very First Stage of disarmament, have successively given ground on this most significant aspect of the armament and disarmament situation. They have now made a proposal whereby the United States and the U.S.S.R. would each keep nuclear weapons and certain connected delivery and defensive systems till the end of the process of disarmament. (76) This last proposal of the Soviet Union has not led to a change in their view that the manufacture of nuclear weapons should cease in the Second Stage of disarmament. But it does make it possible, I believe, to revive meaningful

---

(73) ENDC/2/Rev. 1, dated Nov. 26, 1962, chap. V, art. 22.

(74) ENDC/30, dated April 18, 1962, Stage II, part C, Nuclear Weapons.

(75) James F. Byrnes, **Speaking Frankly,** (New York: Harpers, 1947), p. 273.

(76) A. Gromyko's Statement in the General Debate, 18th Session of the UN General Assembly, dated September 19, 1963.

discussion on the subject of a program for the eventual elimination of nuclear weapons—always assuming that these Powers are able to persuade France and China and others to join in such a program.

There are other weapons of mass destruction: chemical and biological. Article 23 (77) of the Soviet plan calls for their elimination in the Second Disarmament Stage on the same lines as its proposals for the elimination of nuclear weapons. The American plan indicates that the elimination of these weapons could be foreseen in the Second and Third Stages of Disarmament. (78) However, when the Swedish representative suggested that these weapons perhaps could be destroyed on both sides in the First Stage, and their production halted, Charles Stelle said for the United States: "The United States has therefore called for an examination of this problem in the First Stage. In an effort to advance our work still more rapidly we declare our readiness to participate in an expert study group even prior to Stage I. We are, in fact, prepared to begin at any time in order to determine whether measures sufficiently effective and workable can be devised in time to be implemented in Stage I." (79)

Mr. Zorin insisted on linking these weapons with nuclear weapons: "We were at one time prepared to agree to the destruction of these types of weapons at an earlier stage; as you know, the key to the matter is the position of the Western Powers. We believe that nuclear weapons should not be singled out from other types of weapons of mass destruction but should be eliminated during the same stage. Clearly until nuclear weapons have been destroyed, it is extremely difficult to solve the problem of control over the liquidation of chemical and biological weapons." (80)

This could mean that until both sides give up nuclear weapons the Soviet Union wishes to keep in its armory other types of weapons of mass destruction, just in case. It is difficult to see why the final disarmament plan could not accommodate the destruction of these weapons in the very First Stage (as the United States pointed out) but, in view of the Soviet linkage of the matter with nuclear weapons, it seems more likely that there will be no full solution till near the end of the disarmament plan. The non-aligned will continue to press for early action. The expert committee, which the United States suggested might examine the problems of location and destruction of weapons of mass destruction, has not yet been agreed on, much less appointed.

---

(77) ENDC/2/Rev. 1, dated Nov. 26, 1962, chap. V, art. 23.

(78) ENDC/30, dated April 18, 1962, Stage I. A. Armaments par. 4.

(79) ENDC/PV. 37, dated May 15, 1962, p. 13.

(80) ENDC/PV. 36, dated May 14, 1962, p. 41.

Indeed, the Soviet Union has, all through the 18-Nation Conference, tended to regard attempts at the appointment of expert committees as a device to call in science to show that a particular disarmament measure is impracticable. Broadly, they take the view that there must be an unqualified determination and agreement to disarm, and that experts should be called in only when the disarmament treaty is just about ready so as to devise the technical means to resolve such questions of detail as might still exist.

It will be difficult, though not impossible, to find a formula which satisfies the basic requirements of these two rather different points of view. In this sort of issue the nonaligned can and probably will have a role to play. Indeed, on the issue of a nuclear study I suggested that those countries which had made their own studies relating to the destruction of nuclear weapons should make them available to the Conference, for such studies would assist the Committee in deciding what further studies would be required. The British responded to this suggestion and tabled a detailed document entitled "The Technical Possibility of International Control of Fissile Material Production." (81) The immediate reaction of the Soviet delegation was to hail the document as confirming their point of view, because the United Kingdom paper stated that from current production of fissile materials it would be possible to divert secretly 1 to 2 per cent of production, and that it would be possible to falsify figures of past production up to 15 to 20 per cent. Zorin said these figures were intended to establish the Western case for the retention of nuclear weapons and to kill the issue of nuclear disarmament. This was excessive criticism, but the United Kingdom delegate had said, more than once, that he did not see how, taking into account the possibilities of evading controls, the UN Peace Keeping Force to be set up as part of the disarmament treaty and to continue after disarmament could safely be a purely non-nuclear force. We will return to this issue in considering the core problem which I have entitled Peace Keeping Machinery and the Settlement of Disputes.

Though there has been no solution to the issue of the study of methods of ensuring destruction of nuclear weapons and control of fissile materials, the British paper has taken the matter a step further. When I made the appeal that encouraged the presentation of the United Kingdom paper, I also said: "I would refer to the nuclear study which has been proposed. This point figures in the United States plan. Mr. Zorin has told us that the fact that it does not appear in the Soviet plan does not mean that the Soviet Union is necessarily against a nuclear study. This is how I understood him at any rate . . ." (82)

2. *Delivery Systems for Nuclear Weapons.*—This issue, in all its aspects, has taken more of the time of the Geneva Conference than any

---

(81) ENDC/60, dated August 1, 1962 and Corr. 1, dated Nov. 27, 1962.

(82) ENDC/PV. 47, dated June 1, 1962, p. 14.

other single issue. The proposals of the two plans to reduce and eliminate delivery systems are as follows:

The United States plan proposes a thirty per cent cut in Stage I (first three years of the plan) of all major delivery systems. In the Second Stage —the next three years of the plan—there is to be a fifty per cent cut of the remaining delivery vehicles; and in the final and Third Stage (duration of this Stage unstated) the rest of the delivery means are to be eliminated. (83)

The Soviet plan originally called for the complete elimination of delivery systems in the very First Stage of disarmament. This remains the broad pattern of the Soviet plan, but following the statements in the UN General Assembly general debates at the Seventeenth and Eighteenth sessions, the Soviet Union has amended its plan to provide for the retention until the end of the disarmament process of agreed and limited numbers of ICBMs, anti-missile missiles, and anti-aircraft missiles of the ground-to-air type, by the United States and the Soviet Union. Such weapons are to be kept only on the territories of the two countries. (84)

The moves by the Soviet Union are best described as a solid indication that the Soviets now accept the fact that armaments have moved definitely into the nuclear era, and that there is no simple and drastic way of putting the clock back. Diplomatically the moves were surprising. It would probably be an under-estimation to compute that at the Geneva Conference the Soviet delegate and his colleagues from the Socialist countries uttered a half million words in stout defense of the thesis that it was necessary to end the nuclear menace in the very First Stage of disarmament. When the Brazilian delegate suggested that the two sides had not done enough to deal with the problem of nuclear warheads in the First Disarmament Stage, the Soviet delegate offered also to transfer to the First Stage their Second Stage proposals for the elimination of nuclear weapons. Zorin explained that the Soviets were themselves in favor of this but had put the elimination of delivery systems into the First Stage to meet the French view as expressed by General de Gaulle. (85) Thus, one way or another, the Soviets clung tenaciously, from March to September 1962, to the position that the nuclear menace must be destroyed in the First Disarmament Stage.

The first move away from this position, on September 21, 1952 in Mr. Gromyko's statement to the General Assembly, was a surprise. When,

---

(83) U.S. Treaty Outline, March 18, 1962, See Stages I, II and III, Sec. A, Armaments, par. 1 in each case.

(84) Soviet draft Treaty in G.C.D., ENDC/2/Rev. 2, arts. 5 to 8; and A/PV. 1208, Provisional, p. 71.

(85) **Supra**, chap. I, p. 7.

finally, Mr. Gromyko extended the period of retention of certain delivery systems till the very end of the disarmament process, in his speech to the Eighteenth session of the General Assembly, Lord Home, as he then was, speaking as the Foreign Secretary of the United Kingdom, said: "I welcome very much the constructive passages in it (Mr. Gromyko's speech of September 19, 1963) on disarmament, and particularly that passage in which he said that the Soviet Union would be willing to see a certain number of missiles retained on both sides in the Third phase of disarmament. It removes, in my opinion, one of the objections to the proposals of 1962 made by the Soviet Union, and incidentally illustrates the value of discussions in Geneva." (86)

There followed similar, or even more laudatory, comments on the Soviet proposal by the representatives of the "Geneva Conference Powers" in the detailed disarmament discussions in the Political Committee of the General Assembly. (87)

At the Assembly, the United States, however, remained silent about the latest Gromyko move. Charles Stelle, the then Geneva negotiator for the United States, reiterated his Government's position as being one of gradualness, and the reduction of missiles on a percentage basis beginning with thirty per cent in the First Stage of three years. (88)

However, at Geneva, basing himself on President Johnson's letter to Mr. Khrushchev of January 18, 1964, (89) William Foster proposed that the two sides accept and put into operation a freeze on delivery systems for nuclear weapons. On March 2, 1964, Mr. Gromyko criticized (90) the proposal as not being disarmament at all. On March 12, 1964 Adrian Fisher, speaking at Geneva for the United States, said this was playing with words. He said that without a freeze there would be an enormous growth of armaments in the future. The freeze was therefore an integral part of the disarmament problem. He added, "Surely this is disarmament in the most meaningful sense of the word." (91) Semyon Tsarapkin replied that the proposal was control without disarmament and amounted to espionage. (92) If the Soviet record is any guide, the chances of acceptance

---

(86) Records of 18th Session of U.N. General Assembly, General Debate, October 1, 1963.

(87) See speeches of Hassan (U.A.R.), October 28; Burns (Canada), October 29; Sohlman (Sweden), October 30, 1963, in G.A. 18th Session, First Committee.

(88) 18th Session, U.N. General Assembly, First Committee, October 29, 1963.

(89) ENDC/119, dated January 21, 1964.

(90) ENDC/127, dated March 6, 1964.

(91) **New York Times,** March 13, 1964.

(92) **Ibid**

of the U.S. proposal of a freeze, standing alone, is not good. The proposal would appear to involve a comprehensive control of production facilities in both the Soviet Union and the United States, and outside an agreed scheme of disarmament it is very unlikely that the Soviets would accept this.

Also, William Foster has stated that the latest Gromyko proposal was not acceptable to the United States because it would mean abandonment of the U.S. Polaris carrying submarines which are now a very important element in the U.S. defense system. (93) Thus, this important issue of the delivery of nuclear weapons remains unresolved. However, significant developments have occurred which make its resolution much more feasible today than early in 1962. In this sense the Geneva discussions have not been without impact on the issue. I will return to this point in the final chapter of this study.

Another aspect of the issue calls for mention. The United States argues at Geneva that the Soviets are oversimplifying the problem by trying to segregate, for separate treatment, so-called delivery systems for nuclear warheads. While there are, of course, complicated systems for the delivery of nuclear warheads, it is argued that even without the availability of such systems, nuclear warheads could be delivered by transport planes, merchant ships, and some of the artillery systems used for conventional warheads. The Soviets have said that this is just an attempt to undermine their proposal and to evade nuclear disarmament. Our position was that of neither side. I admitted, as did some of the other nonaligned delegates, the possibility of the use as weapon carriers of non-specialized facilities, but expressed the view that this situation could be substantially met by putting a heavier weight of control on those countries (and their allies) which possess nuclear weapons when the treaty of disarmament comes to be implemented. I will deal more specifically with this point below.

3. *Verification and Control of Disarmament Measures.*—In the history of post World War II disarmament negotiations no problem has been more bitterly contested than this one. So much is this the case that it is not even possible to choose a heading for this section without entering the field of controversy. Indeed, this issue is the only one which was not clearly resolved in the Joint Statement of Agreed Principles. There are two letters attached to the Joint Statement of Principles setting out the points of view of the United States and the Soviet Union. In essence the difference concerns the point whether or not verification measures should apply simply to the degree of disarmament or also to the retained arms and forces, so as to ensure that they do not exceed agreed levels at any stage of the disarmament process. The U.S. view is that verification measures

---

(93) ENDC/PV. 165, dated February 11, 1964.

should have the more ample of these two possible coverages, whereas the Soviets say that all they will agree to is a strict interpretation of the wording of the Agreed Principles.

I now deal with this very delicate issue—the most delicate in the disarmament complex—in two stages. First, I look at the positions of the two sides and the third view advanced at Geneva to meet the issue in general. I then look at the specific case of controls with respect to nuclear delivery systems.

On two important points, but not important enough to resolve the issue, there is substantial agreement between the two plans. First, it is common ground that the control measures should be carried out by an International Disarmament Organization to be set up within the framework of the United Nations. (94) The reference to the United Nations is significant, and in itself resolves some issues which could have been very contentious. It means that both the United States and the Soviets envisage the IDO as functioning in terms of the Charter of the United Nations—there is no question of ursurping any of the powers of UN organs, whether the Security Council or the General Assembly. The implications of this important agreement are obvious. I should add that it is also in conformity with number 6 of the Agreed Principles. (95)

The nonaligned without exception welcomed this point of agreement. Indeed, at least one delegation, that of Burma, (96) thought it might be unnecessary to set up additional machinery even within the United Nations. If the IDO is to consist of all the parties to the treaty on disarmament, and since all parties are or will soon be members of the United Nations why not let the General Assembly or one of its committees, function as the IDO? This was the Burmese argument. It has not been pressed. On the whole, the feeling is that as there is agreement on this issue, which does not sidetrack the United Nations, it is best to let it stand.

The second point on which there is agreement is one of substance. This is that all eliminations and reductions are to be carried out under the control of the IDO. (97) Thus, reduction or elimination of armaments will be physically observed. This applies also to the conversion or destruction of plants producing armaments. Again, there has, of course, been no objection to this agreement between the two sides.

---

(94) U.S. Outline: A. Objectives, par. 5, and Soviet draft Treaty, art. 2, par. 3.

(95) See Annex.

(96) ENDC/PV. 56, dated June 16, 1962, p. 42.

(97) Eg, U.S. Outline Stage I, A. Armaments, par. 2(d); and Soviet draft Treaty, art. 5, par. 2.

The unresolved issue between the two sides is whether there should or should not be control over retained arms. The Western position is that such control is essential in order to establish that the agreed disarmament measures are not being circumvented, and, further, in order to check the accuracy of the inventories on which the two sides will base the reductions or eliminations enjoined by the treaty. Thus, the paragraph of the U.S. Outline which I have just cited concludes as follows: ". . . The International Disarmament Organization would verify the foregoing reduction and would provide assurance that retained armaments did not exceed agreed levels." How is the assurance mentioned to be given? Any such scheme would bring in control without disarmament, contend the Soviet delegate and his supporters. What is to stop the United States from beginning with the implementation of the disarmament treaty, check all the retained arms in the Soviet Union and thus obtain a comprehensive picture of the Soviet defense system, they ask. Then the United States could, they say, abandon the rest of the disarmament treaty, because it would possess all target information on the U.S.S.R. In short, contend the Soviet representatives, the Western insistence on checking retained armament would greatly increase, rather than lessen, the danger of war by surprise attack.

The Western reply is that it is just not possible to hazard the security of countries by arms reductions without an accurate notion of what the enemy retains in the way of armament. Here are two of the statements made:

Sir Michael Wright, speaking for the United Kingdom, said: "If there were adequate peace-keeping machinery and an adequate peace-keeping force, there would be little, or at least less, incentive for the hidden retention of arms, for hiding arms 'under the jacket,' and this would surely ease the problem of control." (98)

Mr. Arthur Dean, for the United States, said: ". . . Therefore the United States believes that regardless of whether reductions are effected by agreed numbers of percentages in such sensitive areas, the point is reached very soon where some assurance is needed that the weapons destroyed are not replaced and that no armaments are in fact concealed." (99)

The West, then, sees the problem as one of dealing with concealed or secreted arms. How are they to get the assurance they want? They explained that the logical course would be to make a complete check of the retained arms in the whole territory of each party to the treaty. However, they decided not to insist on such a check, and to be satisfied instead with a "zonal" system of inspections. This system would divide each

(98) ENDC/PV. 43, dated May 28, 1962, p. 10.

(99) ENDC/PV. 45, dated May 30, 1962, p. 11.

country into a number of sectors, each about equal in concentration of military might. Each year the opponent group of countries would select a sector for detailed inspection and spot check. The country being inspected would not know which sector would be selected for inspection by the opposing side. Thus, the United States would pick the zones or sectors to be inspected in the U.S.S.R. and vice versa. The United States suggested that each year 10 per cent of the territory of each country should be subjected to inspection in this manner. Of course, once a sector had thus been opened up to inspection it would remain under inspection—it could not lapse into a closed zone. The only alternative was full verification of the country concerned.

This verification problem arose in its most acute form in connection with the Soviet proposal for a hundred per cent elimination of the means of delivery of nuclear weapons (before the proposal was slightly modified by Mr. Gromyko). General E. M. L. Burns, the Canadian delegate, made a full analysis of the position, (100) and then Joseph Godber, the British delegate, took up the issue in the following terms which spell out fully and clearly the Western position: ". . . as Mr. Burns showed us the other day in his very penetrating speech, this could involve inspectors going all over the Soviet Union. Indeed it could. Mr. Zorin cannot expect us simply to accept his statement that all nuclear delivery vehicles will be put in a certain spot where we can inspect their destruction. He really cannot expect us to accept that statement. Therefore he is complicating the verification issue by trying to push too much of one particular type of disarmament into the First Stage.

"Unless Mr. Zorin says that in putting forward this proposal he is willing for the International Disarmament Organization not only to inspect the spots where the Soviet Union tells us these nuclear delivery vehicles are, but also to inspect such other spots where we think they might be hidden—unless he is willing to give that freedom, in fact he is not promising one hundred per cent verification of the destruction of this particular type of armaments. That is why I say that in bringing forward this proposal in the First Stage he is complicating the verification issue, because this would compel the West to insist on the right to have full inspection over the Soviet Union to ensure that all these particular nuclear delivery vehicles had been destroyed." (101)

The case, then, is one hundred per cent verification of the Soviet Union to accompany the proposed one hundred per cent elimination of nuclear delivery vehicles. This is certainly a logical request. Mr. Zorin's reply was not lacking in interest: "Today you refer to Mr. Burns and asked: 'Do you

(100) ENDC/PV. 30, dated May 3, 1962, pp. 8-11.

(101) ENDC/PV. 31, dated May 4, 1962, p. 47.

agree to the one hundred per cent inspection of the entire territory of the Soviet Union?' I answered you yesterday and I answer you today; as regards verification of the one hundred per cent reduction or elimination of the means of delivery, we agree to such verification throughout the territory of the Soviet Union. What more do you need? ... You, in your plan, wish to reduce the means of delivery by thirty per cent; but you wish to have one hundred per cent verification and keep the bases as well ... and besides, there will be one hundred per cent verification of all means of delivery of nuclear weapons of the Soviet Union without any guarantee that after this thirty per cent reduction you will agree to a further reduction." (102)

Following the Godber and Zorin interchange I made the following appeal to both sides: "I would in a very friendly way make this appeal to both sides. We have heard the defense of their plans. We hope that they are now on the verge of saying to each other, and saying to the Conference, that they are willing to adjust to some extent to each other's plans. There is no point in our hearing further justifications of plan A and of plan B. We know the justifications. But the process of adjustment must start now, and we very much hope that we are on the verge of starting it." (103)

But the appeal went unheeded. The West explained, both at sessions of the Conference and informally, that they were unable to accept the plan of elimination of nuclear delivery means in the First Stage because of the military imbalance that would result, and at that time the Soviet Union was unwilling to budge from its insistence that the nuclear menace must be completely ended in the First Stage of disarmament. The exchanges, however, were not without promise that the problem of verification, immensely difficult though it is, is not beyond solution.

There are, indeed four aspects of the issue of verification to which neither side has yet paid sufficient attention. I drew attention to these aspects at Geneva.

First, both sides might agree that, apart from permitting the production of limited quantities of spares, it would be a logical, and indeed a necessary, part of a sound disarmament program to stop the production of all types of arms in all countries at some point in the first of the Three Stages of the process of disarmament. As a concomitant of this decision there would be a very substantial amount of continuing verification by the International Disarmament Organization. This should be feasible because at Geneva both sides have said or agreed that dismantling or conversion of production facilities would be carried out under supervision, and that

(102) ENDC/PV. 31, dated May 4, 1962, p. 50.

(103) Ibid, p. 53.

there would have to be continued inspection by the International Disarmament Organization to ensure that there was no re-conversion to armaments production, as well as some inspection of other plants which could be converted to such production. All this would add up to a very considerable amount of deterrent control and would bring a considerable degree of confidence that surprise attack could not easily be launched by either side. (The effect would also be felt more widely than just by the two sides to the cold war. One usually tends to refer only to the two sides when it is clear that the context of application is much wider.)

I said something about this aspect of the matter at the Conference session on July 1, 1962: "I would like to point out that surprisingly little has been said in our discussions—surprisingly little—on controls on the reduction and cessation of production of armaments. I would like to draw attention to the fact that this point seems to have been missed. For example Sir Michael Wright on 28 May talked on three categories of verification and he went into some detail about them, but he never once mentioned verification of cessation or reduction of production of armaments: not once. . . . I would submit that we are not getting a complete picture because this point is not being mentioned, and we might, as a result of overlooking this point, tend to exaggerate somewhat the need for other aspects of verification . . ." (104)

I suggest then that the Conference could with advantage examine in greater depth the questions of the elimination of fresh production of armaments and the concomitant verification system, which would have the effect of putting into a wider context the remaining types of necessary verification activities.

Secondly, not enough study has been made of the relationship between the pace of the disarmament plan and the effectiveness of verification measures. This point should be illustrated. If the plan of disarmament is strung out over a long period of, say fifteen years, and assuming that the weight and intensity of control develop slowly, increasing in operative effectiveness as the plan progresses, it is clear that during the earlier stages of the plan there will be a quite considerable scope for evasion by developing production facilities in remote sites or sites carefully concealed from the relatively small numbers of inspectors on a given territory. Therefore, if other relevant matters, such as conversion and employment problems can be ironed out, the plan should move at a rate which is not so slow as to invite evasion of controls. On this aspect of the matter I said at Geneva: "Regarding unlawfully concealed arms or build-up of armaments to replace agreed destruction . . . The slower the advance of the disarmament plan the more complicated this particular problem becomes. . . . We must

---

(104) ENDC/PV. 47, dated June 1, 1962, p. 10.

try and balance and assess the various facts involved in an issue and we must, on that basis, decide on such matters as the pace of our disarmament plan. I would suggest that the complications which arise out of a slow plan are equally facts to be considered by all of us, and I hope that when we come to this question of the pace of the disarmament plan we will take that into account." (105)

Thirdly, the zonal plan having been rejected by the Soviet delegation, and the West too apparently having second thoughts about it—they have not pressed it for over a year at Geneva—I suggested an additional form of confidence creating control which might be *added* to the direct verification of the destruction of armaments, the demobilization of armed forces, the conversion or destruction of production facilities and the continuing checks to ensure that there is no reconversion or other illegal production activity. This additional control would be somewhat on the lines of the invitational plan which the nonaligned included in the Eight Nation memorandum of April 16, 1962 on a test ban. I explained this idea as follows at Geneva: "Our suggestion is that as the disarmament plan progresses it should be feasible for the two sides—in fact for all those engaged in disarmament—to address to the International Disarmament Organization invitations to visit their countries, and to open up in this way from time to time increasingly larger areas of the countries concerned. . . . I would like to put an onus of responsibility on each country. . . . It seems to my delegation that this would be a way of giving an added measure of security to all of us. It would be a measure expressing in the most acceptable form the increasing confidence which we all believe would be an outcome of the development of the disarmament plan as it progressed." (106)

Referring to the above suggestion, Arthur Dean said: "My delegation would be very interested to hear more details about this proposal." (107)

However, as I have already observed, the U.S. delegation did not revert with any emphasis to their zonal scheme, and since my suggestion was conceived as a substitute for that scheme I, too, did not press it further at the time. Perhaps it will, at the appropriate time, be taken up again, and developed by other delegates to the Conference.

Fourthly, the role of observation posts as part of the control mechanism has not been sufficiently developed at Geneva. There is agreement in principle on the utility of limited numbers of these posts, to be set up in

---

(105) Ibid.

(106) ENDC/PV. 30, dated May 3, 1962, p. 26.

(107) ENDC³/PV. 45, dated May 30, 1962, p. 18.

the period before a disarmament plan is agreed on or goes into operation, to counteract the fear of surprise attack. What I have in mind, however, is more extensive use of such posts, once the disarmament plan has got under way, to supplement the other control and verification measures. Such posts could be installed at all airfields of certain specification, on all roads of major importance, at industrial centers and elsewhere. Again, their coverage should increase as the disarmament plan progresses.

Meanwhile the Soviets have shown some flexibility, in a limited but important field, in the matter of the verification of retained arms. Early in 1963, they announced at Geneva that in regard to their proposal of missiles to be retained after the First Stage elimination of the means of delivery of nuclear weapons, they would agree to verification *in situ* of the retained missiles. Semyon Tsarapkin repeated this point, in going over the Soviet proposal, on February 4, 1964. He said: "As regards control the Soviet Government has in mind the fact that during the existence of the 'nuclear umbrella' strict control over it would be established. This control would come into effect from the beginning of the Second Stage of disarmament and, as the Soviet delegation has already pointed out here, the control would be established at the launching pads themselves, and the number of launching pads should not be greater than the number of missiles retained. I believe that no one would dare say that control based on those principles would not be complete. (108)

At a subsequent meeting William Foster, speaking for the United States, did contest the adequacy of the Soviet control proposals. He said: "In the case of verification, for example, the Soviet Union would permit control at the launching pads themselves, at least from the beginning of the Second Stage. We welcome that as a move in the right direction. . . . There has been no indication yet how the Soviet plan would provide assurance against hidden launching pads or vehicles. If, for example, one side suspected that the other was retaining some delivery vehicles in violation of the agreement, what kind of inspection would be allowed under the Soviet proposal?" (109)

Thus, there has been movement, but not enough to resolve the issue. The West does not ask for one hundred per cent verification all through the plan and the Soviet Union has moved a few steps forward. If consideration could be given to retaining agreed numbers of delivery means in the Second and Third Stages of disarmament on the lines of the suggestions contained in the final chapter of this study, and if the four additional types of control and verification measures suggested above can also be utilized, progress should be possible at Geneva on two interrelated and major core problems.

---

(108) ENDC/PV. 163, dated February 4, 1964.

(109) ENDC/PV. 165, dated February 11, 1964.

CHAPTER V

The Remaining Half of the Core

Having dealt with the first three of the Core Problems, it remains for us to turn to the other three, namely: Conventional arms and armed forces; Peace keeping machinery and the settlement of disputes; and Collateral measures or *ad hoc* partial measures in the field of disarmament or arms control.

4. *Conventional Arms and Armed Forces.*—The Geneva discussions have established what might have been foreseen in our nuclear age: the differences over conventional arms and forces have been neither as great nor as time consuming as those on the various aspects of nuclear disarmament.

The U.S. plan calls for a cut of armed forces in Stage I to 2.1 million men for itself and the Soviet Union and, it suggests a formula for the forces of other countries. Arms would be cut 30 per cent in Stage I. In the Second Stage armed forces for the United States and the U.S.S.R. would be brought down to 1.05 million each, and armaments would be cut by 35 per cent of the original levels. In the Third Stage both armed forces and arms would be reduced to the level agreed for final retention by States.

The Soviet plan reduced armed forces for itself and the United States to 1.7 million men in Stage I, and 1.00 million each in Stage II. The difference between these figures and those of the United States is small. Valerian Zorin alluded to this fact as follows:

"We note the United States proposals for Stage II provide for approximately the same level of armed forces for the Soviet Union and the United States. This, of course, is a favorable sign, and the fact that the United States has put forward a similar figure shows yet again how carefully the Soviet Union has considered all the relevant factors in the preparation of its proposals." (110)

Mr. Dean responded:

"I hope he (Mr. Zorin) will judge the merits of his other proposals on the basis of the extent to which they correspond to our proposals. If he

---

(110) ENDC/PV. 40, dated May 21, 1962, p. 29.

does so the prospect is good for the achievement of a far greater measure of agreement on general and complete disarmament." (111)

Mr. Zorin did not continue the exchange to which Mr. Dean prompted him. However, the Soviets did amend their plan so as to bring their figures nearer to those of the United States. For Stage I they raised their figure from 1.7 million men to 1.9 million men. Furthermore, they dropped their proposal of reduction in armament proportionate to the reduction in forces and adopted the U.S. percentage cuts of 30 in Stage I, 35 in Stage II and the remainder to be accomplished in Stage III. (112)

Of course, there remains the fact that the U.S. plan takes considerably longer to implement than the Soviet plan. But here two comments are germane. First, the Soviets have shown that they are not wedded to their original proposal of a four year plan by increasing it to a five year one. Secondly, in the West no final decision has been taken on the length of the plan. The United States outline does not state how long it will take to complete the Third Stage. The British Labour Party has suggested a six year plan.

The one issue which is likely to be highly contentious in regard to armaments and armed forces is their geographical deployment. So far the Soviets adhere to the position that all forces must be withdrawn from foreign territories in the First Stage of disarmament. This is, of course, not acceptable to the West. However, certain changes in the nature of weapons are already affecting the placing of some foreign military bases. The abandonment of the Jupiter and Thor in favor of the Polaris-carrying submarine has led to the closing down of some NATO bases in Southern Europe. Secondly, if eventually it is possible to work out agreed placement of the nuclear umbrellas on the two sides, the American land bases abroad, generally without the means of delivery of nuclear weapons, will not pose any serious military threat to the security of the Soviet Union, even from their point of view. In those conditions it would be difficult to see why the Soviets should maintain *in toto* their present proposal regarding foreign military bases.

Finally, the Soviet argument for the abolition of these bases was that to retain them after all nuclear delivery systems had been eliminated in the First Stage of disarmament (as they then proposed) would give the West a clear military advantage. But this argument is no longer fully valid. The Soviets have moved from their proposal of 100 per cent elimination of nuclear missiles in Stage I to the retention of some missiles till the very

---

(111) ENDC/PV. 43, dated May 28, 1962, p. 15.

(112) ENDC/2/Rev. 1, dated Nov. 26, 1962, arts. II (3) and 24 (2).

end of the disarmament process. Then again, the latest Rapacki plan (113) calls not for withdrawal of forces and arms from Central Europe but for a freeze for the present. This proposal has the support of the Soviet Union and other eastern European Governments. There are thus several indications which point to the possibility of some shift from the original Soviet position at Geneva in regard to the First Stage elimination of all foreign military bases.

5. *Peace Keeping Machinery and the Peaceful settlement of Disputes.*— The first of the agreed principles contained in the Joint Statement sets out the goal of the negotiations. This goal has two parts: the first is disarmament and the second is, "reliable procedures for the peaceful settlement of disputes and effective arrangements for the maintenance of peace in accordance with the principles of the United Nations Charter." (114) The seventh of the eight agreed principles is entirely devoted to spelling out this second half of the dual goal of the negotiations. The great importance of this core problem is, thus, made clear at the very outset.

If the Geneva negotiations do not *appear* to have sufficiently concentrated on the second half of the dual goal this is only partly the case. Undoubtedly the numerous core issues directly concerning nuclear disarmament and its verification have thus far taken most of the time at Geneva; and yet a number of long and deeply probing meetings particularly in April, May and June 1962 were devoted largely or partly to the second half of the goal. However, it is also true that not all the members of the Conference took an active part in these discussions, which were in the main confined to statements by the leaders on the two sides and to my interventions as the representative of India. (115)

The U.S. plan sets out provisions relating to the settlement of disputes and peace keeping machinery in greater detail than does the Soviet plan. However, both sides have provisions on these matters not only in each stage of their plans but also in the preliminary parts of their outlines or draft treaties, preceding the actual stages of disarmament. Thus, in the preliminary part of the United States Outline one of the objectives of the disarmament treaty is stated to be a U.N. Peace Force to be equipped with agreed types of arms. And one of the principles of the treaty is to strengthen the United Nations so as to increase its capacity to insure international security and the peaceful settlement of differences.

---

(113) **New York Times,** March 6, 1964.

(114) See Annex.

(115) Cf. **The American Journal of International Law,** Vol. 57, No. 1, January 1963, pp. 71-72.

Similarly, the Soviet Plan in the preamble reaffirms dedication to the purposes and principles of the UN Charter, and the need to build relations between States on the basis of the principles of peace, good-neighborliness and so forth. Then, in Part I (which precedes disarmament Stage I) it states that only limited contingents of militia will be left with States at the completion of the disarmament plan for the maintenance of international peace and security under the UN Charter and as set out later in the draft disarmament treaty. Furthermore, a very full Article 3 of the Soviet Plan, also preceding the articles dealing with the three stages of disarmament, returns to the obligations of States to maintain international peace and security. It reiterates the UN Charter provisions regarding the abjuring of force in international relations, confirms the resolve of the parties to the disarmament treaty to strengthen the United Nations as the principal institution for the maintenance of peace and the settlement of disputes by peaceful means and contains an obligation on the assignment of forces remaining with States, on the completion of the disarmament process for the maintenance of international peace and security under the United Nations Charter.

In the First Stage of the United States Outline there is a lengthy section entitled, "Measures to Strengthen the Arrangements for Keeping the Peace," (116) which contains obligations similar to those just referred to in the Soviet Plan, and takes three additional steps. The first is to call upon the States Parties to the treaty to undertake a number of studies, e.g., on the codification of rules of international conduct, the strengthening of the means to settle disputes among nations, and on the experience of the UN in regard to peace keeping. The second is to prohibit indirect aggression and subversion, and to study this question so as to assure States against such phenomena. Thirdly, the parties would examine the feasibility of concluding promptly the agreements envisaged in Article 43 of the UN Charter, and they would also conclude an agreement for setting up a UN Force in Stage II of the disarmament process.

The Soviet measures in Stage I are more modestly phrased, partly because the obligations contained in the counterpart American wording is put into pre-Stage I articles, partly because the relevant article does not prescribe studies, and finally because a very definite position is taken up on the creation, via Article 43 of the UN Charter, of the UN peace keeping machinery. Thus, it is laid down that all parties to the disarmament treaty "shall, between signing of the treaty and its entry into force, conclude agreements with the Security Council . . . as provided in Article 43 of the United Nations Charter." The treaty article goes on to state that the armed forces specified for the peace force will be kept in a state of readiness. However, when they are placed at the disposal of the Security

---

(116) ENDC/30, dated April 18, 1962, pp. 17-19.

Council they will serve under the command of the military authorities of the "States concerned." (117)

In the Second Stage of the United States Outline, under the heading "Measures to Strengthen Arrangements for Keeping the Peace," (118) practical steps would be taken to give effect to the studies on the peaceful settlement of disputes, international conduct and prevention of indirect aggression and subversion. Secondly, the United Nations Peace Force would be established. Thirdly, a United Nations Peace Observation Corps would be created, and finally, national legislation would be enacted in support of the disarmament treaty imposing legal obligations on individuals and organizations and providing appropriate penalties for noncompliance.

The Second U.S.S.R. Stage simply says, in a brief article, (119) that the parties to the treaty shall continue to implement the measures already referred to regarding the placing of armed forces at the disposal of the Security Council.

In the final disarmament stage under "Measures to Strengthen Arrangements for Keeping the Peace," (120) the United States plan provides for further steps to ensure peaceful settlement of disputes and peaceful change in a disarmed world, continued codification of rules of conduct, and progressive strengthening of the U.N. Peace Force.

The final Soviet Article (Article 37) goes into some details of the obligations of States in the matter of forces to be made available to the Security Council—their strength and location are to be agreed with the Council—and the command of these units "shall be composed of representatives of the three principal groups of States existing in the world on the basis of equal representation. It shall decide all questions by agreement amoung its members representing all three groups of States." (121)

At Geneva, the United States and the Soviet Union defended their respective concepts. In brief, the U.S. approach is to strengthen the measures contained in the UN Charter (Chapter VI) for the peaceful settlement of disputes, if possible by conducting studies in the subject. It also hopes to place on a more orderly footing the conduct of States in their mutual relations, again on the basis of studies; and similarly it would deal

---

(117) ENDC/2/Rev. 1, dated Nov. 26, 1962, p. 14.

(118) ENDC/30, dated April 18, 1962, pp. 25-26.

(119) ENDC/21/Rev. 1, dated Nov. 26, 1962, art. 27, p. 20.

(120) ENDC/30, dated April 18, 1962, p. 32.

(121) ENDC/2/Rev. 1, dated Nov. 26, 1962, pp. 25-26.

with the matter of indirect aggression and subversion. It is, frankly, not very clear just how these matters would be studied or what results are expected. International studies are extremely difficult to bring to finality when they encompass the views of scores of different countries. Secondly, the United States, while calling for an examination of the feasibility of prompt action under Article 43 of the UN Charter, seems to set up a United Nations Peace Force outside this article of the Charter. On this point Arthur Dean said at Geneva:

"Either we develop effective institutions for settling international differences and keeping the peace, or we in effect abandon our hopes for general and complete disarmament. . . . In the field of keeping the peace, the parties would (in the U.S. Plan) agree to support measures for strengthening the effectiveness of the United Nations." (122)

About a month later he added the following:

"We have heard a good deal from our Soviet colleague, to the effect that the United States plan seeks to bypass the United Nations. Nothing could be further from the truth; indeed, I welcome the statement made by the representative of India on that point this morning. On the contrary, the United States wishes to strengthen the United Nations by creating a United Nations peace force which can guarantee effectively the rights of States as set forth in the Charter of the United Nations. Mr. Zorin has stated on many occasions that Article 43 of the Charter of the United Nations provides the means for establishing forces which may be used by the Security Council, but this certainly does not mean that members of the United Nations may not agree to create institutions such as the United Nations Peace Force which may be necessary in order to safeguard, in a world of general and complete disarmament, their fundamental rights under the United Nations Charter. Article 43 of the United Nations Charter does not exhaust the means provided in the Charter to ensure the collective security of Members of the United Nations . . ."(123)

Mr. Zorin reacted strongly:

"If we give our agreement to the setting up of an international force, why should our agreement to the creation of this force not be based on Article 43? What difference would there be? In either case the agreement of all the Permanent Members of the Security Council is necessary. If you obtain our agreement to the setting up of an armed force in a certain form this agreement will be in accordance with Article 43 also . . . If

---

(122) ENDC/PV. 40, dated May 21, 1962, p. 11.

(123) ENDC/PV. 55, dated June 13, 1962, p. 41.

you wish to do this without our agreement, you will be acting in opposition to us. But can you conclude a treaty on general and complete disarmament against our opposition? It is quite clear that this is unrealistic." (124)

There are other important unresolved points. Mr. Joseph Godber of the United Kingdom suggested certain principles which should apply to the composition and other arrangements relating to the UN peace force. He attacked the idea of the troika command proposed by the Soviet Union, and also the possible application of Security Council vetoes. Mr. Zorin counterattacked these principles sharply:

"Do you want to give the command to a single individual, who would inevitably be a representative of the Socialist countries, or the Western Powers, or the nonaligned States? It is of course clear to everyone that in such a case armed forces could be used against the interests of any of the groups of three States and to the detriment of their security." (125)

Mr. Godber argued in favor of the UN peace force being equipped with nuclear weapons, even when the disarmament process had been completed, so as to be able to deal with a case of concealed nuclear weapons or other contingencies. This too Mr. Zorin strongly opposed, as did many of the nonaligned to whom the idea of giving the UN force the power to use atomic weapons appeared excessive. On this point the U.S. position was unexceptionable to most of the countries at the Conference. Mr. Dean said:

"We provide that whatever contingents remain to the national forces for peace keeping work inside their own territories shall not be armed with nuclear weapons. Then we say that the United Nations peace force should be armed with 'agreed weapons' but that it ought to be strong enough to be able to keep the peace in the world and to put down any violations of the peace of the world by any country. . . . My Government has an open mind on this question." (126)

Speaking for India, I analyzed both plans in detail and made some suggestions. Regarding the basis of the peace force I said:

"It is a matter of regret that Article 43 of the United Nations Charter has not been implemented, and I think we must bind ourselves clearly and strongly to implement that Article and thus create the international peace

---

(124) Ibid, p. 56.

(125) ENDC/PV. 55, dated June 13, 1962, p. 59.

(126) ENDC/PV. 45, dated May 31, 1962, p. 37.

force, which seems to be intended in the United States plan but which is set out in a manner which is not sufficiently strong. I hope in the plan we finally adopt we can be much clearer on this matter." (127)

In regard to indirect aggression and subversion I suggested that this "matter should rather be dealt with *ad hoc,* as and when cases arise, as was done in Laos." (128)

On the United States idea of national legislation in support of the treaty on disarmament, I said:

"We are wholly in favor of and welcome that idea. I have compared this with the Soviet plan in which I found two or three references to national legislation supporting, for example, the elimination of nuclear weapons, the cessation of military training, and so on. But we think it would be preferable on the whole to have one omnibus clause regarding national legislation as proposed in the United States plan." (129)

Regarding the type of command which the Soviet plan advocates I said:

"While we are glad to see that the wording of the Soviet draft adds up to the fact that the international peace force will be a force, we are of the opinion—tentatively at any rate—that the suggested method of command would be extremely difficult to implement in practice. We would imagine that this would certainly require further thinking." (130)

I summed up the Indian position as follows:

"We think that the United Nations peace force is more or less common ground and that agreement could be reached on its manning, on its armament—a very important matter—on its stationing and on its command.

"So far as other matters are concerned, some studies are proposed by the United States. Our view is that these studies should be undertaken in the light of and in conformity with the corresponding United Nations Charter provisions so as to make it quite clear that we are not side-stepping the United Nations.

---

(127) ENDC/PV. 55, dated June 13, 1962, p. 22.

(128) Ibid, p. 23.

(129) Ibid, p. 24.

(130) Ibid, p. 25.

"Regarding the matter of peaceful settlement of disputes, which is the third point in my concluding remarks, I should like to say that both plans agree that peaceful settlement should be in accordance with United Nations procedures. The United States, in addition, introduces the International Court of Justice . . . while we agree with the idea in principle, we find that it will not shift the practical factors very much unless the International Court of Justice can be made much more acceptable to the world community of States.

"Fourthly there is the question of international rules. We would make the suggestion that these should be developed *ad hoc*, as in the case of Laos, rather than by a somewhat abstract study.

"Fifthly, there is the United States suggestion about peace observation. We think this is already provided for and can be operated under the Charter of the United Nations, and that it may not be necessary to spell this out again.

"Sixthly, we welcome the idea of national legislation in support of the treaty. We would strongly support it." (131)

Finally, I drew attention again to "the suggestions I have made for a pragmatic, *ad hoc* approach to the settlement of some questions which will arise. We hope that that can be borne in mind." (132)

I led on to a conclusion about our present needs:

". . . from the Hague Conventions of 1899 and 1907 until the commencement of World War II, there had been negotiated some 300 Conventions, bilateral and multilateral, for the pacific settlement of disputes—Conventions which, I believe, are still in force. This is a most striking fact because it most clearly emphasizes that what was lacking when we came to the mid-thirties was not the means for peaceful settlement of disputes—there were these 300 international Conventions—but general and complete disarmament under international control. Those 300 agreements for the settlements of disputes are still there. What we do not have—the missing piece in our whole situation—is general and complete disarmament under international control . . . and that is what we must supply." (133)

It is clear that the Soviet ideas keep closer to Chapter VII of the UN Charter than do those of the West. The latter are skeptical of the Soviet

---

(131) Ibid, pp. 26-27.

(132) Ibid, p. 27.

(133) Ibid, p. 28.

approach after the long period of failure to implement Article 43 of the Charter. This is, to say the least, understandable. On the other hand the Soviet plan provides that the agreements under Article 43 must be concluded between the signing of the treaty on disarmament and its coming into force, i.e. before the commencement of the process of disarmament. In other words, if there is no compliance with this part of the treaty there will be no disarmament. It is most doubtful that the Soviets would go through the whole process of negotiating a disarmament treaty with the West and with the nonaligned countries and then jettison the whole process by failure to implement the clause on the creation of the UN Peace force which they themselves have made a condition precedent to implementation of measures of disarmament.

On the questions of the composition of the force and its command I find myself strongly of the view that it will not be possible to take general decisions such as the appointment of a commander for a period of years. The commander of the Force will have to be chosen with reference to the operation concerned. Thus, in the Congo operation the Secretary-General had to take into account the strong sentiment of African member States that the command should be largely African. In the Gaza strip it would not have been possible to give the command to a Western European. It went first to General Burns of Canada (who then became Canada's delegate to the Geneva disarmament conference), and next to General Gyani of India. In Cyprus the parties directly involved have apparently accepted General Gyani. Thus, each case has to be decided taking into account the prejudices, policies, and alignments of the countries concerned. This will have to continue. Similarly, the composition of the Force has, in each case so far in UN history, been decided in consultation with the country in whose territory it has had to function. This too will be broadly necessary in the future. However, each party to the disarmament treaty will earmark various units, keep them in a state of battle readiness, under commanders acceptable to the United Nations, and armed and located in agreement with the United Nations; and perhaps the Secretary-General might keep a roster of possible commanders for UN peace keeping operations which could be approved either formally or informally by the Permanent Members of the Security Council, or by the Council itself.

What of the financing of the Force when it is used for UN operations? If the Force is constituted in terms of Article 43 of the Charter, and is used in accordance with Security Council decisions, there would be no serious difficulty about financing. However, in the future as in some recent UN operations, it might be desirable to make *ad hoc* financing arrangements by agreed contributions from the countries directly concerned. At any rate, such a system might be appropriate in a particular case and should be not ruled out for occasional application. But the Force will probably or possibly not be used exclusively in pursuance of Security Council resolutions. The Council might fail the world in a situation in which aggression had to be curbed. In such a case the precedents at the United Nations of resorting to the Uniting for Peace Resolution (number 377 V of November 3, 1950) will be the best guide to action. In order to make it financially possible to launch such action—and indeed action under Security Council authorization pending the working out of financial arrangements for it—the United Nations might set up a UN Peace Operations Working Fund of say $50 million on the basis of agreed contributions. As and when agreed drawings take place the Fund should be replenished by further contributions on the prescribed scale. I believe it might be possible to get the membership of the United Nations to accept the need for such a Fund provided it would be used only in accordance with Security Council resolutions, or resolutions of the General Assembly, and only pending the working out of the definitive financial arrangements for the operations concerned, unless it is agreed that a particular case falls within the normal administrative budget of the United Nations.

One of the remaining issues is the type of arms to be used. The United Kingdom has made a powerful plea for some nuclear arms for the UN Force. At Geneva they are in a minority in this view. The question, however, has to be faced squarely. What if some country does conceal a cache of nuclear war heads? Or what if some highly developed country should decide it was not being fairly treated in the disarmed world and should secretly build itself some deadly weapon? Should the United Nations not be in a position to meet such eventualities? The answer would have to be yes, *provided* only that it can be shown that there are no ways of ensuring that these circumstances will not arise.

At present there is no known scientific way of ensuring that all the world's nuclear warheads are located and destroyed. While this is true, it does not follow that a country which managed to secrete some of its bombs would ever be able to make them an effective threat. I frequently said at Geneva that the weight of controls will have to be much heavier in those countries which now possess nuclear weapons than in countries which do not possess them. For example, every ship or aeroplane which leaves the harbors and airports of such countries will have to be carefully searched to ensure that no nuclear weapons are on board, and launching of outer space vehicles will have to be carefully supervised from the same point of view. This would be an inevitable aftermath of the present state of the world. Secondly, the weight of controls will have to be heavy also in a country which, though not possessing the nuclear weapon, is obviously in a position to manufacture it. I would suggest that the possibilities of such controls be carefully considered and that even if they are onerous they be accepted before taking any decision to retain nuclear weapons for the UN Force.

The strongest reason against the British position is that if it were decided to place a number of nuclear bombs at the disposal of the United

Nations I am afraid that some countries might be tempted to prepare themselves for the eventuality of the United Nations deploying those weapons by secreting more bombs than were assigned to the United Nations. In short, a decision to give the United Nations nuclear weapons would be a strong incentive to cheating. Whereas if the United Nations were not to have such weapons, and if the weight of controls were made adequate to the circumstances of each country—and the additional control and verification measures which I have suggested in this study were to be adopted—I believe it would on balance be in the interests of the world, and more likely to ensure peace, if there were a decision not to keep any nuclear weapons and to go all out in locating and destroying all of them and in making it senseless for a country to try to secrete them. In any case, if it were decided to keep a few bombs for the United Nation, the problems of location of such weapons, their proper custody and guarding from capture by anti-social elements would probably be more difficult to solve than the problem of effective controls to locate, destroy, or neutralize existing stocks.

6. *Collateral Measures or* ad hoc *Partial Measures in the Field of Disarmament or Arms Control.*—These are the tension reducing, confidence creating, disarmament facilitating measures referred to in the second paragraph of the Conference's procedural decision of March 28, 1962. (134)

The Conference has given one meeting a week, on the average, to consideration of these measures, or rather and much too frequently, to consideration of which of these measures should be discussed. Thus, in March and April 1964, we witnessed a battle of weeks between the preference of the West for discussion of a verified freeze on the numbers and characteristics of strategic nuclear offensive and defensive vehicles, and the preference of the Soviets and their allies for discussion of percentage reduction of military budgets. The nonaligned delegates have suggested parallel discussion of both, or some other combination of the 13 possible collateral measures which might be discussed. There are five such proposals in President Johnson's statement to the Conference, which Mr. Foster read into the record at Geneva on January 21, 1964, (135) and nine proposals in the Memorandum of the Soviet Government which Mr. Semyon Tsarapkin read to the Conference on January 28, 1964, (136) the non-dissemination proposal being found in both documents.

However, it is in this general field that the Conference has so far achieved some tangible results. Its long discussions of test ban possibilities led, finally, to the Moscow treaty of August 1963. A few months

---

(134) **Supra,** p. 13.

(135) ENDC/PV. 157, dated January 21, 1964, pp. 10-12.

(136) ENDC/PV. 160, dated January 28, 1964, pp. 5-10.

previously the United States and the Soviet Union negotiated at Geneva a direct communications link between Washington and Moscow—an element under the wider heading, "Reduction of the possibility of war by accident, miscalculation, or failure of communications," which was an agenda item proposed by the United States at the Conference. And at the Eighteenth Session of the UN General Assembly came the unanimous adoption of a resolution prohibiting the orbiting of weapons of mass destruction—again a tension reducing measure originally proposed at Geneva by Canada.

Since the partial test ban was originally, and again in the proposals of the United States and the United Kingdom at Geneva on August 27, 1962, a Western proposal, all the three proposals in this field so far adopted were originally Western. This is not accidental. Though both sides have proposed agenda items under the heading of collateral measures in my view the West has, generally speaking, been more interested in such measures than the Soviet Union, which has repeatedly emphasized that its main, and almost its sole interest at the Conference is to reach agreement on general and complete disarmament.

Over a two and one half year period somewhat more than twenty proposals have been put to the Geneva Conference under the general heading of collateral measures, but it has seldom been easy to agree on consideration of any among them. Indeed, the item on the non-orbiting of weapons of mass destruction never was agreed upon by the co-chairmen of the Conference as one for full consideration. However, Canada, Mexico, Italy, India and one or two other delegations repeatedly spoke about it as an item on which agreement should be reached in order to preserve outer space from becoming part of the arena of the cold war. At first the U.S.S.R. opposed the general idea on the ground that outer space could not be thus insulated until it was agreed that all missiles should be eliminated. This is because long range missiles enter outer space in their trajectory. However, the General Assembly resolution (137) evades this issue by confining itself to the question of the orbiting, or placing in outer space, of weapons of mass destruction.

At the Geneva Conference the discussion of partial or tension reducing measures serve the important function of probing areas in which relatively minor but nevertheless significant agreements might take place. In this way advantage can be taken of a degree of detente, which may not be great enough to result in a major step such as disarmament, but which may nevertheless yield some results. Without these probings, and the possibilities they bring to light, the sterility of the task of the disarmers at Geneva would probably prove to be intolerably frustrating. I like to refer

---

(137) G.A. Res. 1884 (XVIII), dated October 17, 1964.

to these measures, and the attempt to agree on them, as a recurring exchange of credentials of good will and re-affirmation of intent. Apart from their wider purposes, this is a very important and helpful one.

At the same time, it would be incorrect to lay too much store by this aspect of the work at Geneva. Indeed, it must not be overlooked that partial measures are generally of such a nature that they do not have the inherent capacity to endure for long unless they are backed by fuller measures, and eventually probably by the process of disarmament itself. The partial test ban could, in the event, serve to illustrate this point. Unless its prohibitions are extended to cover all tests of nuclear weapons—including underground tests—it is unlikely that the partial test ban will continue indefinitely. It could break down in a few years if, say, France and China insisted on carrying out extensive series of atmospheric tests which some of the other Powers felt were, in fact, revealing new possibilities for nuclear weapons. It could also break down if one side, more than the other, were to carry out intensive series of highly successful underground tests which were yielding important weapons advantages.

If the partial test ban could be converted into a comprehensive test ban, then its life might be somewhat more secure, but the present mood of France and China would jeopardize the continuance of even a comprehensive test ban. In fact, both Governments have made it clear that they will not consider abandonment of testing of weapons till the super Powers agree to embark on nuclear disarmament itself. It would be an error to consider this attitude as a French or Chinese aberration. So long as there are nuclear weapons in the world there will be a widespread feeling among the nations that there is no secure defense today, other than such weapons themselves, of their vital interests. If, in short, nuclear deterrence is the method which the super Powers feel serves best their vital interests, then why should others with vital interests to consider be content with a second or third class defense of those interests?

This feeling, and growing conviction, is the reason why no agreements among the super Powers on the non-dissemination of nuclear weapons will secure the world against proliferation of such weapons. Such agreements could succeed in delaying the spread of nuclear weapons by a few years. Definitive agreement at Geneva to put this issue on the active agenda of items to be discussed was not reached till June 18, 1964. It has been discussed, to some extent, off and on, ever since India proposed it in March 1962, but not systematically. The super Powers are now keen to come to agreement on it, and last year, though not at Geneva and yet influenced by the discussions there, they agreed at Vienna that the International Atomic Energy Agency would not give out fissile materials to any country except under Agency safeguards. Until that time the Soviet Union had been backing the stand of India and other countries that it would be unfair and not meaningful to burden the less developed countries with onerous and expensive safeguards against the diversion of fissile materials to non-peaceful purposes when the countries which could or were likely to embark on weapons programs would not go to the Agency for assistance in setting up research or power reactors.

Since the I.A.E.A. decision, taken with both the United States and the Soviets concurring, there has been a greater likelihood of agreement being reached at Geneva to discuss the matter of non-dissemination. The subject is the one item which figures both on President Johnson's list of five proposals contained in his statement read to the Conference on January 21, 1964, and the Soviet Government's proposals read to the Conference on January 28, 1964. However, there is a significant difference in the concepts of the two sides which has prevented the item from being the first choice of either for the immediate agenda before them. This difference is that the Soviet proposal makes it explicit that "transfer of nuclear weapons or access to them shall not take place indirectly, through military blocs, for example, through the so-called multi-lateral nuclear force of Nato." (138) On the other hand, the U.S. proposal would prohibit transfer only to "the national control of States which do not now control them." (139) This difference is presently so fundamental that it is thought impracticable to push the question of the non-dissemination of nuclear weapons into first place in the agenda at Geneva.

The question of priority among the items on the potential agenda is significant in that it indicates the directions in which, at a particular moment, each of the two sides wishes, or considers it practicable, to move. When NATO started to debate seriously the possibility of a multi-lateral nuclear force the Soviet Union, which had hitherto not pressed the item, pushed to the first place as its choice for the agenda (in the collateral measures field) the item on non-dissemination, which India had originally suggested to the Conference. I might remark that in the early stages of the Geneva Conference I drew up the text of a proposed agreement on th subject of nondissemination of nuclear weapons, and, with the approval of the Government of India, I handed copies to the United States and Soviet delegations. From time to time we inquired whether they had formulated their positions on our proposals. After a lapse of many months we were told that the two super Powers were discussing the matter bilaterally, as they both wanted to reach agreement on the issue; however, they did not wish it to be discussed at the Conference. We welcomed these bilateral efforts and did not seek to push the item at Geneva. Our purpose was to stimulate the process of consideration by those directly concerned. Later, the Soviet Union pressed for the item being placed on the agenda, but there was no agreement to do so. This is a case where both sides would

---

(138) ENDC/PV. 160, p. 9.

(139) ENDC/PV. 157, p. 12.

like to come to agreement, both favoring an increase of mutually agreed activities to constrict the size of the nuclear club. But full discussion is still barred by the problem of whether the creation of multi-national nuclear forces should or should not be regarded as dissemination of nuclear weapons.

The interest in a particular type of collateral measure can shift remarkably fast. The question of the use of force to change frontiers and demarcation lines illustrates this point. As recently as December 31, 1963 (140) Mr. Khrushchev thought this matter so urgently important that he wrote to many heads of State about it. President Johnson wrote back expressing the interest of his Administration in the proposal, and suggesting its enlargement to deal with the question of attempts to change boundaries, whether by the use of force or indirectly such as by the clandestine supply of arms. President Johnson presumably felt that his response on this issue justified his mentioning it as the first of the five points which he considered that the Geneva Conference could take up when it reassembled on January 21, 1964. (141) However, surprisingly, the nine suggestions of the Soviet Union for urgent measures, presented a week later, did not even include the issue raised by Mr. Khrushchev less than a month previously. The Soviet Union was still interested in the matter but it had slipped in priority. It rated only a brief perfunctory mention at the tail end of Mr. Tsarapkin's speech to the Conference on January 28, 1964. It is difficult to see why this should be. The suggestion has its relevance to the German problem, as does the issue of a NATO multilateral force to which the U.S.S.R. continues to assign high priority.

In choosing for top priority the reduction of military budgets, it would seem that the Soviets are demonstrating to their own people and to their Eastern European allies that they are going to make a big effort to get the Federal Republic of Germany to cut back the recent increases in its defense budget. Recently Mr. Tsarapkin contended at Geneva that that Government's military expenditure had tripled in the last ten years and now accounts for 34 per cent of its over-all expenditures. (142) If there is no general endorsement of this view at Geneva—the Indian delegation has pointed out that the circumstances of a country might be such that it is compelled to increase its military spending—the Soviets will probably move to another in the long list of pending items relating to tension reducing measures.

Another example of an item in which both sides are interested, but which has never been simultaneously pressed vigorously by both of them,

(140) **N.Y. Times,** January 4, 1964.

(141) ENDC/120.

(142) ENDC/PV. 166, dated February 13, 1964.

is the setting up of observation posts in Europe to decrease the dangers of surprise attack. On March 19, 1962, at the very commencement of the Geneva Conference, the Soviets included this matter in a memorandum on various measures which they presented at the Conference. However, they did not mention it again in the next year or so. Meanwhile the United States took it up among the measures they would like to see adopted to reduce the risk of surprise attack. But the Soviets were pressing at that time for measures such as a denuclearized zone in the Mediterranean area, and other forms of disengagement in Europe. Then, late in 1963, the Soviets returned to the idea, combining it with the thinning out of forces in Central Europe, a position which has again been modified and brought nearer the actualities of negotiation by the latest version of the Rapacki plan. So the slippery game of agreeing on priorities continues.

It thus appears that tension reducing or collateral measures only come within the scope of real negotiation when the timings of both sides coincide regarding the priority to be assigned to a particular measure. This has occurred twice or thrice in two years—not a spectacular pace, but still one which makes for at least a modest contribution to the relaxing of the cold war confrontation.

CHAPTER VI

The Prospects for Disarmament

There will be virtually no prospects for continued negotiation or agreements in the general field of disarmament and arms control unless two minimal assumptions can be fulfilled.

The first assumption is that both the United States and the Soviet Union will remain at least as strongly convinced as today that it is worthwhile to strive for the creation of an international security system, rather different from the present one which has come to be based on the existence, on either side, of massive destructive power. I believe the reasons which implanted this conviction will remain operative: they stem from the appalling dangers inherent in the prevailing system of world security. Indeed, on February 27, 1964, William Foster, speaking for the United States at Geneva, pointed out that U.S. strategic missile inventories have increased more than two hundred per cent since the Conference first convened two years ago and that unless the arms race can be arrested they will reach, in 1965, approximately seven hundred fifty per cent of the March 1962 level. (143)

These dimensions of destructive power do not bring security with confidence. However, it will still require steadfastness of purpose on the part of the world leaders if there is to be an effective impetus for disarmament. A very close and distinguished observer of the Presidency of this country has written: "Unless a President uses these powers with energy, arms control agreements are improbable. The momentum of the arms race— the power at work to keep it going almost without conscious new decision —is enormous. Military men in all countries find it hard to approve any arms control proposal which is not either safely improbable or clearly unbalanced in their own favor. In the United States only a strong Commander-in-Chief with a strong Secretary of Defense is in a position to press steadily for recognition that the arms race itself is now a threat to national security." (144)

The same is undoubtedly true in Moscow and in other significant capitals. We must hope for continued steadfastness for disarmament, the reasons for which remain enormously potent. In this chapter I will assume that this is the case.

---

(143) ENDC/PV. 170, dated February 27, 1964, p. 48.

(144) McGeorge Bundy. **"The Presidency and the Peace,"** Foreign Affairs, April 1964, p. 362.

The second basic assumption that must hold if there is to be a real prospect of disarmament and arms control is that there will be no marked deterioration in the relationship between the United States and the Soviet Union. Irritations there will be, causing ugly flashes and dark trails of smoke, but these will not necessarily wreck disarmament negotiations. However, certain events in Europe, on either side of the dividing line, could change the basic mood, and then our second assumption could be negated. It is impossible to assess the chances of such a negation. I do not see such developments around the corner; I think both sides, within their understanding of the demands of their respective vital interests, would strive to avoid them; I think the habit of more effective communication between the United States and the Soviet Union is catching on and spreading—slowly. In these circumstances, for the purpose of the remarks that follow, I will take it that this second assumption will be broadly operative.

One more point should be added in regard to these assumptions. We must expect times when neither will be at its peak point of operation. These ups and downs will not affect the basic willingness to proceed with disarmament negotiations, but they might well influence the tactics, priorities, and flexibility of one side or the other. This factor bedevils any assessment of the immediate prospects for disarmament, and it must be borne in mind as a possible brake or tangential force which at any moment could retard or distort such constructive momentums as might develop.

At Geneva there is a danger of overdoing a certain trend, which is to concentrate overmuch on collateral or tension reducing measures. This is a reversal of the situation which existed in 1962, when the main effort at the Conference was to explore basic problems connected with substantive disarmament—of course, accompanied by measures of international verification. A good deal of attention was also given to the test ban issue.

In 1963 there were, it might be said, special reasons for concentrating on measures other than a plan for general and complete disarmament. First, in the aftermath of the Cuban crisis, it was natural that there should be a searching look at each other's credentials, i.e., an examination of mutual willingness to take small confidence re-building steps, which is what collateral measures essentially are.

Secondly, the year commenced with an almost irreversible concentration on the question of a test ban, a major collateral measure. When the Conference reopened at Geneva in January 1963, after the Seventeenth session of the General Assembly, the feeling was very strong, particularly among most of the nonaligned delegates, that the test ban issue had to be solved before there could be meaningful talk on general and complete disarmament. It took until August 1963 to get the partial test ban. Then came the

Eighteenth session of the UN General Assembly, and the Conference reconvened on January 21, 1964 at Geneva with three collateral measure agreements on the assets side.

Was this not adequate re-affirmation of credentials and of mutual good will? One could have hoped so, and yet both programs of urgent measures placed before the Conference by the two sides—by the United States on January 21 (145) and by the Soviets on January 28 (146)—dealt almost exclusively with collateral measures. The only item which perhaps does not fully belong to this category is the elimination of all bomber aircraft, (147) which is the eighth of the nine Soviet proposals. But the Soviets propose it on the ground that all such aircraft are now obsolete. They contend that the elimination would fit the facts, would diminish the risks of war, and would reassure both sides of mutual willingness to move forward to substantive steps to reduce non-obsolete effective military power.

It would seem that, by and large, the concentration of 1963 on collateral measures will continue during 1964. Perhaps an underlying reason is that this is a Presidential election year. Countries have come to feel that in an election year it is not realistic to expect major moves by the U.S. Administration, and new substantive disarmament proposals would probably fall within this category. I am not trying to assess whether in fact the United States is unable to make fresh proposals on disarmament in 1964. My point is that I doubt that any of the more seasoned negotiators at Geneva expect such moves this year. If they were to be made they would come as a surprise to the Geneva delegates. Thus the area of possible agreements in 1964 probably is again largely restricted to collateral measures.

While the realities of political forces would seem to lead to this conclusion, I would also draw attention to three other realities, all of positive interest in relation to disarmament and arms control. One is that President Johnson is continuing to prepare public opinion in the United States for moves away from the older concepts of security. On March 24, 1964, for example, speaking at Washington to the National Legislative Conference of the Building and Construction Trades Department of the A.F.L.-C.I.O. the President said: "The world has changed and so has the method of dealing with disruptions of the peace. . . . In a matter of moments you can wipe out from 50 to 100 million of our adversaries or they can, in the same amount of time, wipe out 50 to 100 million of our people, taking half of our land, half of our population in a matter of an hour.

---

(145) ENDC/PV. 157, pp. 11-12.

(146) ENDC/PV. 160, pp. 5-10.

(147) This is also true of the U.S. proposal for the destruction of a certain number of U.S. and U.S.S.R. bombers.

"So general war is impossible and some alternatives are essential . . .

"My most fervent prayer is to be a President who can make it possible for every boy in this land to grow to manhood by loving his country— instead of dying for it." (148)

These remarks are pertinent to, though not directly, the attitude of the United States towards arms control and disarmament. More directly relevant is the study ordered by the President into problems connected with the conversion of the U.S. economy from one significantly dependent on military spending to a full peace time one. (149) There are, thus, indications that it is not necessarily the policy of the United States Administration to make proposals exclusively to arrest the arms race, or to counteract the dangers of suprise attack, but rather to move to active negotiations on substantive disarmament.

A second reality which is in a sense complementary to the first is that, while the negotiating Powers at Geneva and the whole body of the United Nations in general will not expect vigorous and practical disarmament negotiations before the American Presidential election, they will certainly expect such negotiations immediately thereafter. It may be assumed that the Nineteenth session of the UN General Assembly will adopt unanimously or nearly so, a resolution calling on the Powers directly concerned, and whatever disarmament negotiations may be planned, to get on vigorously with the preparation of an agreed blueprint for general and complete disarmament. In short, there will be strong opposition to the tendency of concentrating on collateral measures at Geneva. There will be insistence on genuine disarmament negotiations.

Should, however, concentration on collateral measures have become a settled habit, tending to carry over into the post-Presidential election period, I can see the 18-Nation Conference bringing to bear on the two sides all the pressure it can muster so as to move them into negotiations on substantive disarmament. It might well be that, if the two sides are unable to find mutually acceptable compromises on the basis of their disarmament plans, the nonaligned will consider it necessary to present a third plan, or make detailed proposals on the core issues.

Indeed, next year I foresee the presentation of fresh proposals to solve the most important of the core problems—those relating to nuclear disarmament, control and verification measures, and peace keeping arrangements. Some of these proposals might be made even earlier, so as to give

---

(148) **New York Times,** March 25, 1964.

(149) **New York Times,** March 26, 1964, (The Committee on the Economic Impact of Defense and Disarmament.)

the two sides time to consider them. There are certain to be some suggestions made at the next session of the General Assembly, in addition to searing criticism of the great Powers, and also of the other members of the 18-Nation Disarmament Conference, for not yet having got anywhere with the resolving of the key problems of disarmament.

The main effort will be to find the basis for agreement on the reduction and eventual elimination of the vehicles for the delivery of nuclear warheads. There is now agreement that these vehicles are to be retained by both sides till the end of the process of disarmament; and there is also agreement that reduction should start in the very First Stage by taking off a considerable slice. The point of dispute is how large that slice should be, and how verification procedures would ensure implementation of the agreed cut. There is also the question of the composition of the complement of retained vehicles.

We might take first the last of the above matters—the types of the vehicles to be retained. The response of the United States to the latest Gromyko proposal is that the types suggested for retention are too limited. Specifically it has been stated, ". . . it would apparently eliminate in that Stage (the First Stage) nuclear delivery vehicles upon which the West has come to rely more than the Soviet Union seems to. Those eliminated include, for example, missile launching submarines." (150) I would suggest that it is likely that a compromise proposal would provide the retention also by both sides of agreed numbers of Polaris carrying submarines. If the West makes a similar case for the retention of another type, or other types, of vehicles, they too could be considered for retention. It would be best of all, from a negotiating point of view, for the compromise proposal suggesting the retention of submarines (and possibly other categories of vehicles), in addition to the categories already mentioned in the Gromyko proposal, to be made by the nonaligned countries. It would then be for the two sides to react.

As to numbers: the Gromyko proposal is that in Stage I all delivery means be destroyed except agreed numbers which would provide a nuclear "umbrella" till the end of the disarmament process. The numbers are not stated. Another question arises. Did Mr. Gromyko mean that the same number would be retained by the two sides? And that in each category the number would be the same on either side, and furthermore that in all retained categories there would be one and the same figure of retention on the two sides? The answer is that none of these kinds of equality has been asked for in the Soviet proposal. On the contrary, in a recent statement on this subject at Geneva, Semyon Tsarapkin invited the West "to indicate a certain figure or figures at this stage (of the debate). . . ."(151)

---

(150) ENDC/PV. 165, dated February 11, 1964, p. 42.
(151) ENDC/PV. 163, dated February 4, 1964.

This was a fairly clear invitation to inequality, which would suit the West much better than equality. Indeed, in other ways the Soviets have made it known that they would not expect the West to suggest equal figures. The second element of a nonaligned compromise proposal could be to invite the two sides to state their figures for retained vehicles, taking into account the present figures and their assumed ratio. In short, I do not believe that any figures should be suggested by the nonaligned, certainly not in their first effort at a compromise proposal. In order to get agreement the two sides should negotiate the figures bilaterally, if this is at all possible.

But the agreed sizes of umbrellas to be opened at the end of the First Stage of the disarmament process do not exhaust questions of figures. The next question is whether the umbrellas should be larger through the Second Stage than through the Third Stage. On the whole I think it is not illogical to make do with a smaller umbrella when the weather improves, which it should do as the disarmament process continues and the weight of verification measures increases. Presumably the Second Stage umbrella would have to be about twice as large as the Third Stage one, and if the umbrella principle, based on agreed types of vehicles and warheads comes to be accepted, I do not think it will be a major difficulty to get agreement on the reduction of the sizes of the umbrellas for the Third and Final Stage of disarmament.

One more word about the figures on which the sizes of the umbrellas would be based. The Institute for Strategic Studies in London estimates Western superiority in ICBMs in the early part of 1964, as almost five to one. (152) This superiority is in number of vehicles. On the other hand, the U.S.S.R. ICBMs are shown with a megatonage some three to eight times as high as that of the Western weapons. This would seem to show, that, even if the numbers to be retained were to bear some relationship to the ratios of the ISS figures for the numbers of weapons available to the two sides, the U.S.S.R. will not be far behind the United States in the megatonage of its weapons. Thus, the present rough balance of strength could be preserved.

What of verification measures? These are of course crucial, but in my view they cannot be considered in isolation for this question of vehicles alone. The problem of verification is, to a large degree, a problem of confidence. It is, therefore, a total problem, one that concerns the disarmament plan as a whole. The reduction of the means of delivery of nuclear weapons and their final elimination will be but one of several or many aspects of the continuing process of disarmament. Verification must be

---

(152) The Institute for Strategic Studies, London, **The Military Balance, 1963-64s,** pp. 34-35. The figures for Fleet Missiles are about 2 to 1 in favor of the West (numbers, not megatonage).

viewed over all against the total disarmament plan. I have already indicated in this study that there are unsolved verification problems of great importance. I have suggested four additional control measures to deal with them. I draw attention to those measures (153) again, in connection with a possible compromise proposal for dealing with the issue of vehicles for the delivery of nuclear weapons which has been developed in outline in the preceding paragraphs of this study.

A third problem on which attention is being increasingly focused is that of peace keeping arrangements. The nature of modern weaponry has brought us into the era not of preventive wars but of the prevention of wars. Or as Ambassador Adlai Stevenson said in his Hammarskjold Memorial Lecture at Princeton, on March 23, 1964, this is an age of the peaceful settlement of disputes. (154) On this subject too, I have already made suggestions in this study, (155) the purpose of which is to furnish the United Nations with adequate strength together with flexibility. Two additional suggestions might be considered. One is that the two sides, and indeed all countries which seek to develop the new international order, should not balk at opportunities of extending the area of international peace keeping. I take two specific examples. First, the situation between India and Pakistan. There has been an unfortunate re-occurrence of shooting—using not just small arms—on the cease-fire line in Kashmir. Why should the two countries concerned not be encouraged to seek a strengthening of the UN Truce Observance team? Indeed, if the situation further deteriorates, the Security Council could act in this sense on the initiative of one of its own members, or the Secretary-General could make a reference to the Council under Article 99 of the UN Charter. It might be desirable also to extend observation to other parts of the frontier between the two countries.

Another example is the case of Cambodia. If the arrangements which Cambodia desires in order to ensure its neutrality and independence can be made, and it would seem that one way or the other the demand in this respect of Cambodia will be met, then it should be followed by strengthening the International Commission which now observes the 1954 Geneva Accords on Indo-China. Indeed, rational settlements in Southeast Asia will tend to be related closely to international peace keeping machinery for some time to come.

My second suggestion is more basic, and I believe it is timely. There is increasing emphasis on the need to strengthen international peace keeping machinery. This need is recognized by both super Powers, even if not equally by the two of them. However, there have recently been two unani-

---

(153) **Supra,** pp. 48-51.

(154) **New York Times,** March 24, 1964.

(155) **Supra,** pp. 60-62.

mous votes in the Security Council of the United Nations on the setting up and continuance of a peace keeping force in Cyprus; (156) and there is some evidence that the Permanent Members of the Security Council would probably prefer to revive the United Nations Charter role of the Council in the realm of peace keeping rather than see it exercised by a very large and increasingly unpredictable General Assembly.

There is an effective and practical way of demonstrating that this is so, to which thought could be given. This would be to take up again now the long abandoned efforts to implement Article 43 of the United Nations Charter, and to seek to reach the agreement or agreements prescribed by that Article on the contingents of armed forces to be made available to the Security Council by member States for peace keeping operations. Both the United States and the Soviet disarmament plans envisage exploration of the possibility of implementation, or the very early implementation, of the provisions of Article 43 of the UN Charter. Why should examination of this issue await agreement on a disarmament plan? The carrying out of the provisions of Article 43 is an existing UN Charter obligation, which has remained frustrated but which should not be any longer deferred. The climate is more conducive now to the implementation of the provisions of the Article than it has been for the last fifteen years.

If the Permanent Members of the Security Council would consider this suggestion, we might see the emergence of a most significant development, and one which would give a very great impetus to the work of the 18-Nation Conference. The implementation of the provisions of Article 43 of the UN Charter, apart from being a major practical step to strengthen the United Nations, would be one of the biggest developments in the realm of collateral or tension reducing measures that could be achieved. Such implementation would not raise problems of ratification by governments. They have already ratified the UN Charter which calls for this action.

I have been looking into the future—not the very distant future, for that would be pure speculation—but more or less at possibilities in 1965. The bridge to that period could possibly consist of one or two more tension reducing or collateral measures, though there will be considerable criticism in some UN quarters that the third year of disarmament negotiations, on the basis of the agreed Principles of September 20, 1961 (Annexed) has failed to start producing results in the field of substantive disarmament measures. What are the prospects for another agreement or two in the general area of collateral measures? Non-dissemination, in spite of suiting the basic mood of both the United States and the Soviet Union, seems unlikely for the present in view of the problem of accommodating the multi-lateral force project. A non-aggression pact comes up directly against

---

(156) Security Council Resolution of March 4, 1964, (text in **New York Times,** **March 5, 1964**), and Security Council Resolution of June 20, 1964 (text in **New York Times,** June 21, 1964).

the question of recognition of the German Democratic Republic by the West. The freeze on nuclear delivery vehicles would seem to pose quite considerable problems of verification. But there are new forces, to which I have drawn attention, tending toward reduction or a cut-off of the production of fissile materials for weapons. The phasing out of bombers will probably be resisted until these vehicles are all due to be phased out by unilateral action on either side, but this will probably not be the case for the next few years. However, there might be agreement to dismantle some B47s and TU16s.

In my opinion the immediate effort should be directed also to three other issues. One is the completion of the test ban treaty by its extension to underground tests. Perhaps the nonaligned should go back to a plan on the lines of the one which they did not introduce about a year ago. (157) If the test ban could be thus completed it would add something substantial to the present discouragement of the 5th to the Nth countries in the development of the bomb. This objective is in keeping with the desire of both sides to arrest the dissemination of nuclear weapons.

The second issue worth probing further is the revised Rapacki plan. It proposes a freeze instead of a thinning out of weapons and forces in an area where a freeze is likely to take place anyway. To formalize it would give some assurance of a stabilized position. Some awkward problems could be avoided by the NATO countries entering into an international agreement among themselves to freeze the military position in a certain agreed area for the next five years (or longer), and registering the agreement as an international treaty under Article 102 of the Charter of the United Nations. The Warsaw countries could simultaneously register with the United Nations a similar treaty among themselves on a certain area on their side of the line—it would run for the same period as the NATO treaty, and contain precisely similar provisions. Indeed, the two treaties would be international twins. The UN Member States concerned could also, if they so wished, make statements about the treaties on the UN record, in the General Assembly or the Security Council, or in both.

Side by side with the above there could be work directed to a system of observation posts: a third issue well worth exploring. On the basis of a freeze it becomes more practicable to work out an observation system than under schemes of reduction. The scheme would be easier because it could be a relatively modest one. Assuming that it was operated with meticulous strictness in terms of the agreement reached it would serve a most valuable confidence building purpose. Again, it should be possible to devise diplomatic methods for setting up the arrangements which would avoid awkward problems for either side.

---

(157) **Supra,** pp. 24-25.

Work on the foregoing three lines, in addition to consideration of cessation of fissile material production for weapons and bonfires of bombers, even if all of them do not come to the stage of formal agreements during the current year, would be a constructive use of the time of the Conference. It is also possible that further voluntary unilateral action might promote progress on the reduction of military budgets.

Though there will probably not be any agreements this year in the area of substantive disarmament I do not for a moment wish to be construed as suggesting that there should be no discussion of problems relating directly to disarmament. It would not be only bad tactics to turn aside from the discussion of disarmament, as distinct from collateral measures, and thus cause resentment at the United Nations, where the Conference would be charged with breach of terms on which the Assembly endorsed the setting up the 18-Nation Committee by resolution number 1722 XVI of December 20, 1961. (158) Discussion and clarification of positions help to reveal possibilities on the major issues. Besides, there are issues which have so far been discussed rather sketchily in a "first round" of debate. These include the important issues of peace keeping machinery and the general problem of verification measures—the latter would, of course, also be discussed in connection with specific disarmament measures.

There must, in particular, be a free and frank exchange on the question of weaponry for the peace keeping force. The various aspects of the matter have not yet been sufficiently exposed. The discussion will not at this stage be conclusive, but consideration in depth would be useful. Meanwhile, there will be at least one more UN operation in peace keeping to provide additional data to the negotiators: the delicate and difficult one in the Island of Cyprus.

---

(158) **Supra.** See footnote 21.

Joint Statement of Agreed Principles for Disarmament Negotiations

Having conducted an extensive exchange of views on disarmament pursuant to their agreement announced in the General Assembly on 30 March 1961,

Noting with concern that the continuing arms race is a heavy burden for humanity and is fraught with dangers for the cause of world peace,

Reaffirming their adherence to all the provisions of the General Assembly resolution 1378 (XIV) of 20 November 1959,

Affirming that to facilitate the attainment of general and complete disarmament in a peaceful world it is important that all States abide by existing international agreements, refrain from any actions which might aggravate international tensions, and that they seek settlement of all disputes by peaceful means,

The United States and the USSR have agreed to recommend the following principles as the basis for future multilateral negotiations on disarmament and to call upon other States to co-operate in reaching early agreement on general and complete disarmament in a peaceful world in accordance with these principles.

1. The goal of negotiations is to achieve agreement on a programme which will ensure that (a) disarmament is general and complete and war is no longer an instrument for settling international problems, and (b) such disarmament is accompanied by the establishment of reliable procedures for the peaceful settlement of disputes and effective arrangements for the maintenance of peace in accordance with the principles of the United Nations Charter.

2. The programme for general and complete disarmament shall ensure that States will have at their disposal only those non-nuclear armaments, forces, facilities, and establishments as are agreed to be necessary to maintain internal order and protect the personal security of citizens; and that States shall support and provide agreed manpower for a United Nations peace force.

3. To this end, the programme for general and complete disarmament shall contain the necessary provisions, with respect to the military establishment of every nation, for:

   (a) Disbanding of armed forces, dismantling of military establishments, including bases, cessation of the production of armaments as well as their liquidation or conversion to peaceful uses;

   (b) Elimination of all stockpiles of nuclear, chemical, bacteriological, and other weapons of mass destruction and cessation of the production of such weapons;

   (c) Elimination of all means of delivery of weapons of mass destruction;

   (d) Abolishment of the organization and institutions designed to organize the military effort of States, cessation of military training, and closing of all military training institutions;

   (e) Discontinuance of military expenditures.

4. The disarmament programme should be implemented in an agreed sequence, by stages until it is completed, with each measure and state carried out within specified time-limits. Transition to a subsequent stage in the process of disarmament should take place upon a review of the implementation of measures included in the preceding stage and upon a decision that all such measures have been implemented and verified and that any additional verification arrangements required for measures in the next stage are, when appropriate, ready to operate.

5. All measures of general and complete disarmament should be balanced so that at no stage of the implementation of the treaty could any State or group of States gain military advantage and that security is ensured equally for all.

6. All disarmament measures should be implemented from beginning to end under such strict and effective international control as would provide firm assurance that all parties are honouring their obligations. During and after the implementation of general and complete disarmament, the most thorough control should be exercised, the nature and extent of such control depending on the requirements for verification of the disarmament measures being carried out in each stage. To implement control over and inspection of disarmament, an International Disarmament Organization including all parties to the agreement should be created within the framework of the United Nations. This International Disarmament Organization and its inspectors should be assured unrestricted access without veto to all places as necessary for the purpose of effective verification.

7. Progress in disarmament should be accompanied by measures to strengthen institutions for maintaining peace and the settlement of international disputes by peaceful means. During and after the implementation of the programme of general and complete disarmament, there should be taken, in accordance with the principles of the United Nations Charter, the necessary measures to maintain international peace and security, including the obligation of States to place at the disposal of the United Nations agreed manpower necessary for an international peace force to be equipped with agreed types of armaments. Arrangements for the use of this force should ensure that the United Nations can effectively deter or suppress any threat or use of arms in violation of the purposes and principles of the United Nations.

8. States participating in the negotiations should seek to achieve and implement the widest possible agreement at the earliest possible date. Efforts should continue without interruption until agreement upon the total programme has been achieved, and efforts to ensure early agreement on and implementation of measures of disarmament should be undertaken without prejudicing progress on agreement on the total programme and in such a way that these measures would facilitate and form part of that programme.

Letter from John J. McCloy, United States Representative at the US-USSR Exchange of Views on Disarmament, to V. A. Zorin, Deputy Minister of Foreign Affairs of the USSR

20 September 1961

Dear Mr. Zorin:

At the 18 September 1961 session of our bilateral discussions on disarmament you indicated that the draft of a joint statement of agreed principles which I submitted to you on behalf of the United States Government on 14 September 1961 would be acceptable to the Government of the Soviet Union provided the following clause were omitted from paragraph 6;

"Such verification should ensure that not only agreed limitations or reductions take place but also that retained armed forces and armaments do not exceed agreed levels at any stage."

This sentence expresses a key element in the United States position which we believe is implicit in the entire joint statement of agreed principles that whenever an agreement stipulates that at a certain point certain level of forces and armaments may be retained, the verification machinery must have all the rights and powers necessary to ensure that those levels are not exceeded.

It appears from your statements that the Soviet Union will be unwilling to agree to a joint statement of agreed principles unless the above-mentioned clause is omitted therefrom. My Government has authorized me to inform you that, in the interests of progress toward resuming disarmament negotiations, it is willing to remove the above-mentioned sentence from paragraph 6 of the joint statement of agreed principles since it is an item to which the Soviet Union has not agreed.

This is done upon the express understanding that the substantive position of the United States Government as outlined in the above-quoted sentence and in our memorandum of 14 September 1961 remains unchanged, and is in no sense prejudiced by the exclusion of this sentence from the joint statement of agreed principles.

The United States continues to adhere to and will continue to advance the principle contained in the omitted sentence as a necessary element in any comprehensive disarmament negotiations or agreement.

Very truly yours,

(Signed)   JOHN J. MCCLOY

Letter Dated 20 September 1961 Addressed by the Representative of the USSR In the USSR-United States Bilateral Negotiations On Disarmament to the Representative of the United States In the Negotiations

Dear Mr. McCloy,

I have received your letter of 20 September 1961, in which you express a reservation with regard to the position which the United States of America intends to adopt in subsequent negotiations on disarmament.

According to the agreement which we reached in the course of a bilateral exchange of views, the United States agreed not to include, in the joint statement by the Governments of the USSR and the United States on the principles for disarmament negotiations, the proposal with which you are conversant and the adoption of which would imply acceptance of the concept of the establishment of control over armaments instead of control over disarmament. In your letter you say that this proposal "expresses a key element in the United States position."

In this connexion I must state that, as you know, the position of the USSR on the question of control over general and complete disarmament has been thoroughly and clearly explained in the statements of the Soviet Government and its leader N. S. Khrushchev. The Soviet Union favours the most thorough and strict international control over the measures of general and complete disarmament. While strongly advocating effective control over disarmament and wishing to facilitate as much as possible the achievement of agreement on this control, the Soviet Union is at the same time resolutely opposed to the establishment of control over armaments.

It appears from your letter that the United States is trying to establish control over the armed forces and armaments retained by States at any given stage of disarmament. However, such control, which in fact means control over armaments, would turn into an international system of legalized espionage, which would naturally be unacceptable to any State concerned for its security and the interests of preserving peace throughout the world. The position of the United States on this question, if it insists on the proposal described above, will inevitably complicate agreement on a programme of general and complete disarmament, on the general principles of which we have agreed.

The Soviet Union will continue to make every effort towards the earliest preparation of a treaty on general and complete disarmament under effective international control.

I have the honour to be, etc.

V. Zorin

*Permanent Representative of the USSR
to the United Nations*

INDEX